NATURE
AWAITS

SCIENCE
IN THE WILD

ENJOY NATURE

52 FUN PROJECTS AND ACTIVITIES TO EXPLORE, DISCOVER, AND LEARN FROM NATURE

ERICA L. COLÓN, PhD
FOUNDER OF NITTY GRITTY SCIENCE

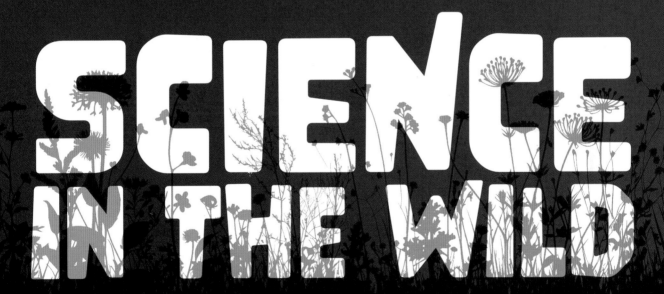

SCIENCE IN THE WILD

QUARRY

Quarto.com

© 2024 Quarto Publishing Group USA Inc.
Text © 2024 Dr. Erica L. Colón

First Published in 2024 by Quarry Books, an imprint of The Quarto Group,
100 Cummings Center, Suite 265-D, Beverly, MA 01915, USA.
T (978) 282-9590 F (978) 283-2742

Quarry Books titles are also available at discount for retail, wholesale,
promotional, and bulk purchase. For details, contact the Special Sales Manager
by email at specialsales@quarto.com or by mail at The Quarto Group, Attn:
Special Sales Manager, 100 Cummings Center, Suite 265-D, Beverly, MA 01915, USA.

10 9 8 7 6 5 4 3 2 1

ISBN: 978-0-7603-9006-1

Digital edition published in 2024
eISBN: 978-0-7603-9007-8

Library of Congress Cataloging-in-Publication Data
Names: Colón, Erica L., author.
Title: Science in the wild : 52 fun projects and activities to explore,
   discover, and learn from nature / Erica Colón.
Description: Beverly, MA : Quarry Books, an imprint of the Quarto Group,
   2024. | Includes index. | Summary: "Science in the Wild is a captivating
   activity book that combines science and adventure through 52 simple,
   hands-on activities anyone can do right outside their front door"--
   Provided by publisher.
Identifiers: LCCN 2024012555 (print) | LCCN 2024012556 (ebook) | ISBN
   9780760390061 (trade paperback) | ISBN 9780760390078 (ebook)
Subjects: LCSH: Natural history--Experiments--Juvenile literature. | Nature
   study--Juvenile literature.
Classification: LCC QH55 .C65 2024 (print) | LCC QH55 (ebook) | DDC
   508--dc23/eng/20240423
LC record available at https://lccn.loc.gov/2024012555
LC ebook record available at https://lccn.loc.gov/2024012556

Design: Cindy Samargia Laun
Photography: Teresa Busch and Erica L. Colón
Illustration: Creative Market / Cutessy,
   except Ada Keesler on pages 21 and 29 and Shutterstock on page 37

Printed in China

TO THE FEARLESS DOZEN:
Ava, Dani, Lincoln, Caitlynn, Ryleigh, Reagan,
Cole, Paisley, Avori, Beau, Elleary, and Aubrey.
May your days be filled with endless sunshine,
muddy trails, and boundless laughter. This book is
dedicated to your wild spirits and the joy
you bring to every adventure!

CONTENTS

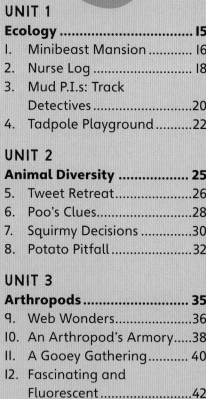

PART 1
LIFE SCIENCE 13

INTRODUCTION

Science in the Wild is an engaging collection of investigations that will not only take you into the most incredible science lab—the outdoors—but will also have you answering essential science questions through discovery and exploration in nature. Through the investigations and

challenges in this book, you will learn to use inquiry skills, including manipulating materials, observing, gathering data, and creating models, just as scientists do. These skills will allow you to successfully investigate essential questions, make discoveries, and experience the immersive world of science in the wild.

WHY LEARN IN THE WILD?

Science isn't confined to a classroom—it's a method for exploring the natural world around you. Science of the natural world is classified according to three main types: life science, which deals with living things; earth science, which studies the planet Earth and space; and physical science, which focuses on things with energy and matter, the stuff that makes up everything.

Heading into the wild, also known as the great outdoors, you can now access all the sciences in a natural lab setting. Wild exploration may include studying animals, plants, rocks, weather, flight, and other aspects of the natural world. The best part is that you may encounter something unexpected or a natural phenomenon during your experiments. These are the best surprises and will likely lead to more discoveries.

Science in the Wild is a journey to transform how you learn science. While learning online and in the classroom are important, it's just as essential to go outside to connect nature with science, and to immerse yourself in that world. I can guarantee you'll discover and see wondrous things you'll never find in a textbook. Invite your family to join you in these adventures and witness the wonders of nature together!

CONCRETE JUNGLES ARE WILD TOO

Urban environments with their many roads, buildings, and other artificial structures are called "concrete jungles." These environments do not usually come to mind when discussing the wilderness or the great outdoors. Nevertheless, you would be surprised to learn about all the wild spaces and microhabitats that thrive in urban environments. Some of my favorite adventures of learning science in the wild came from pockets of nature in the bustling city.

When you are in an urban environment, start exploring wild spaces in nearby parks, green areas, waterfronts, and community gardens. Talk with your family and invite them to visit local botanical gardens and arboretums, or take an excursion to explore nature reserves and wildlife sanctuaries, which often have educational programs and tours.

THE SCIENCE AND NATURE CONNECTION

Studying science in an untamed environment allows us to observe and understand the natural world directly.

This connection means that when scientists venture into the wild, they're not just studying facts in a textbook or conducting experiments in a controlled setting—they're immersing themselves in the dynamic and sometimes unpredictable physical world of living things, ecosystems, and geological formations. This hands-on approach helps them better understand how all the elements of nature interact and influence one another.

Moreover, it reminds us that nature is the ultimate laboratory to test theories, make discoveries, and grow our understanding of the world in ways we cannot replicate indoors.

USER'S GUIDE TO THIS BOOK

The investigations and activities presented in *Science in the Wild* are arranged by science disciplines: Life Science, Earth Science, and Physical Science. You can start in a science discipline you like the most and explore from there, or you can conduct investigations in any order. In some cases, the seasons of the year may be your only limitation.

Each investigative lab has an easy-to-follow format so you can complete it independently. Some steps may need a grown-up's help, indicated by difficulty levels.

Each activity introduces a problem in the form of an **Essential Question** that you should be able to answer upon completion of the activity. Sometimes the activity is designed for more open-ended opportunities, so the question may be more challenging.

The **Difficulty Level** is listed for each activity to help you understand the rating of of the challenge. You are more than capable of completing all activities. Read through all materials and steps before you begin any investigation. If you are unsure of anything, ask a grown-up, who will be happy to guide you to ensure success! The difficulty ratings are as follows:

- **Easy:** Simple experiments or challenges using commonly available materials that can usually be done independently, without adult help or supervision.
- **Moderate:** Experiments may involve slightly more complex procedures and may need adult help for safety or guidance in one or more steps.
- **Advanced:** Experiments that involve stricter procedures or more precise measurements that may require adult supervision or assistance for safety and execution.

The **Materials** section lists all the materials needed to conduct the investigation. Although these are nature-based activities, you will need some materials found within your home to perform the investigation. Please get permission to use any of these materials, ensure that everything is clean, and when done, return items to where you found them. Great scientists always clean up after themselves.

Each investigation provides a step-by-step **Procedure**. Diagrams or illustrations are sometimes included if further explanation is needed on a technique or step.

Each investigation offers an opportunity to **Take It Further** by suggesting additional activities or variables to extend learning.

The investigations wrap up with **Explore the Science**, breaking down each activity's concept and real-world context.

Do you want to know something really wild? Each investigation or challenge relates to facts and phenomena in the real world. Check out the section labeled **Now, This Is Wild!** to see each relevant connection!

SAFETY CONSIDERATIONS

Safety is always an essential part of science investigations. By following safety guidelines, you create not only a safe environment but an enjoyable one as well. If there is a step you do not understand, ask a grown-up for help.

The investigations in *Science in the Wild* always keep safety in mind. Before beginning any experiment or challenge, check for the safety symbols related to the activity. These safety symbols will signal you to follow specific safety precautions. The following symbols will alert you to potential hazards and precautions:

SCIENCE IN THE WILD

Sharp Object Safety: Scissors or other tools used for cutting should always be used as directed. Always direct the sharp points or edges away from yourself.

 Physical Safety: When an experiment involves physical activity, take precautions and follow directions to avoid injuring yourself or others.

 Plant Safety: Handle plants carefully. If you're unsure about a plant, ask a grown-up for help with identification. Always wash your hands when you are done handling plants.

 Animal Safety: Treat live animals with care to avoid harming them. Always return animals where you found them. Always wash your hands when done handling animals.

 Breakage Safety: If you are working with breakable materials, like glass, handle them carefully. If something breaks, ask an adult to help you clean it up.

 Heat Safety: Some investigations use objects that produce heat or apply heat or flames. Do not touch hot objects with your bare hands—wear heavy gloves.

 Eye Safety: Eye protection is mandatory to avoid injury.

 General Safety: This symbol is used if no other symbols specifically apply but still require general caution.

HEADING INTO THE FIELD

When scientists head outdoors to conduct investigations, they say they are heading into "the field." Good scientists will tell you they never go into the field without their trusty field bag. To assemble your field bag, grab an old backpack (not the one currently holding your homework) or a grocery bag and add some essential supplies:

- Water
- Sunscreen
- Bug repellant
- Magnifying lens
- Ruler
- Lab notebook
- Pencil
- Colored pencils
- Healthy snacks wouldn't be a bad idea, either

Besides these essentials, you also want to check the materials list for each investigation. Please return any material list items borrowed from around your home to their original place when done with your activities. Also, remember the golden rule when outdoors—leave nothing but your footprints, and take nothing but pictures. Consideration for nature is essential for all the *Science in the Wild* activities. Respecting and preserving the delicate balance of the natural world ensures our experiments yield meaningful results while minimizing any potential environmental harm. This means not leaving trash or materials behind, not disrupting habitats, and being mindful of the area around you.

PART 1
LIFE SCIENCE

Life science, also known as biology, is the study of all living things, which involves exploring life on a global scale across the entire planet down to the microscopic world of cells and bacteria. Life science also includes studying the diversity of organisms that live on Earth through the discovery of nature and investigative approaches that aim to explain nature.

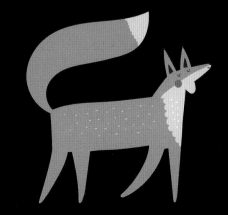

UNIT 1
ECOLOGY

Ecology is the study of organism interaction and their environment. Become a budding ecologist to examine living and nonliving relationships. Create a Minibeast Mansion, a temporary retreat for nature's critters. Prepare for a close encounter with a Nurse Log to discover that a rotting log is more than meets the eye. Become a Mud P.I. and learn who's been visiting certain areas by sleuthing out their tracks. Witness the incredible life cycle of an amphibian by creating a Tadpole Playground. It's time to gear up with your field bag and explore the astonishing world of ecology!

1

MINIBEAST MANSION

A minibeast is a small creature like an insect, spider, worm, or other tiny invertebrate that can be found in various types of habitats, from gardens and forests to puddles and ponds. Studying minibeasts will help you understand how they interact with each other and within their preferred environment.

ESSENTIAL QUESTION

How do different habitats support the diverse communities of minibeasts?

PROCEDURE

1. Find an area to design your minibeast mansion, away from a lot of human activity and near vegetation like flowers or small trees. Your space should be about 24 × 24 inches (60 × 60 cm).
2. Divide your space into four separate "rooms" for the minibeast mansion. If you don't have a ground area, make the rooms using trays or flowerpots.
3. Use materials to create the following "rooms" *(See Figure 1)*:
   - **The Woodland Retreat**—create a room of sticks, bark, small pieces of logs, and firewood to create a rustic atmosphere.
   - **The Earthy Hideaway**—add loose, clean soil for those creatures seeking a comfortable and debris-free dwelling.
   - **The Meadow Oasis**—plant some grass seeds to offer a fresh, vibrant space that insects and invertebrates can call home.
   - **The Stonework Sanctuary**—stack stones, fragments of pavement, or broken bricks to provide robust, small spaces.

DIFFICULTY LEVEL: **Moderate**

SAFETY:

MATERIALS

- Untreated wood (sticks, firewood, building scraps)
- Soil
- Grass seed
- Variety of rocks, broken bricks, or pavement
- 4 plastic trays or flowerpots (optional)
- Natural items (pebbles, pinecones, seeds, etc.)

Figure 1: Create rooms in the minibeast mansion.

EXPLORE THE SCIENCE

The mansion's environments mimic natural habitats. Observing interactions between living organisms and their environments reveals how specific conditions and resources influence the distribution and behavior of minibeasts. This first activity lays the groundwork for future exploration in ecology. Visit weekly to observe the various changes among the plants, animals, decomposers, and the environment.

NOW, THIS IS WILD!

Biosphere 2 was an expensive science experiment in Arizona that tried to copy the original Biosphere (Earth) inside a giant glass dome. Eight people lived inside for two years with many plants and animals from five different biomes: mangroves, tropical rainforest, savannah grassland, desert, and ocean. The original project failed due to loss of oxygen. However, small experiments are still ongoing at the facility to better understand climate and climate change.

4. Over the next week, watch as new "guests" start arriving. Keep a record in your journal and see if preferences change as new guests arrive or habitats change.

5. You can maintain your mansion for an extended time by keeping it slightly damp, cutting grass to about 4 inches (10 cm) tall, and carefully returning rocks and logs after lifting them to observe the minibeasts beneath.

TAKE IT FURTHER

Add additions to your mansion. For example, you can add a small carpet remnant—soak it in water and place it down as a new room to see what moves in underneath. Or you can add a small garden of flowers or herbs and see if it attracts pollinators or caterpillars.

2.

NURSE LOG
· ·

Even when trees are no longer alive, they help the forest. Nurse logs are fallen trees that slowly break down, allowing new plants to grow and providing a microecosystem for other living things. These logs give shade, nutrients, water, and protection to the young plants, just like a nature nursery for the next generation of trees.

ESSENTIAL QUESTION
What organisms live and survive on a decomposing log?

DIFFICULTY LEVEL: **Easy**
SAFETY: ✚ 🐾

MATERIALS
- Tools for digging (plastic knife, spoon, tweezers, craft stick)
- Small flashlight
- Magnifying lens
- Small clear jar
- Insect identification book (optional)

PROCEDURE
1. Look around outside your home or ask an adult to hike in a local forested park to look for fallen trees that have already started decaying or rotting.
2. Walk around the nurse log and look closely for clues of living organisms on the surface (*See Figure 1*):
    - Fungus or mushrooms
    - Moss
    - Broken seeds
    - Seedlings
    - Animal holes
    - Lichen
    - Ferns
3. Use your digging tools and carefully pull off rotting bark or pull apart wood fibers (*See Figure 2*), and use your flashlight and magnifying lens to look closely for clues of organisms living inside the nurse log:
    - Insects
    - Centipedes
    - Worms
    - Small amphibians like frogs, salamanders, or newts
    - Snails
4. Use your tweezers to collect organisms and place them in your jar to observe them.
5. Record your observations in your science journal. You can use an insect identification book to figure out which bugs you've seen. Use drawings and labels to mark where you found everything on your nurse log. When you're done observing and recording, remember to return them to the same place you found them.

SCIENCE IN THE WILD

18

Figure I: Look for living organisms on the nurse log.

Figure 2: Pull back the bark and look through layers of the nurse log.

TAKE IT FURTHER

Return to the nurse log throughout the year and measure how it deteriorates while the saplings and new plants grow. Continue to record any observations of new life and growth on the nurse log through the seasons.

NOW, THIS IS WILD!

Fungi, which include mushrooms, are important decomposers, especially in forests. However, there is one humongous fungus found in Oregon that is the largest living thing on Earth! This one fungus breaks records, covering an area of 3.5 square miles (9 km²)!

EXPLORE THE SCIENCE

Trees, like all life, succumb to wildfires, lightning, windstorms, and insect infestations. Once fallen, they decompose, or break down, with the help of microorganisms, such as fungi and bacteria, and other decomposers, such as worms and mushrooms. Over time, holes are formed and filled in with soil, moss, and little plants carried by wind or small animals. This rich soil, called humus, is full of nutrients that support new plants. As time goes by, small animal species will use the nurse log as a home and continue to enrich the humus with additional fertilization with their food debris and poo.

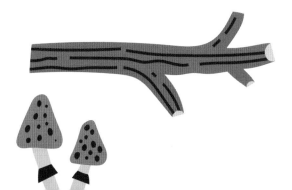

3. MUD P.I.s: TRACK DETECTIVES

Uncover the secrets of the wildlife that roam around you by setting up your track station. Observe and document footprints left behind by various animals after using tracking techniques and creative baiting.

ESSENTIAL QUESTION
What is a method for documenting the behavior of animals in their natural habitats?

DIFFICULTY LEVEL: **Moderate**
SAFETY: ✂ 🐾

MATERIALS
- Large garbage bag
- Large rocks
- Mud (dirt and water)
- Bucket
- Shallow tray
- Peanut butter, birdseed, or fruit and vegetable scraps
- Track ID guide (*See Figure 1*)
- Scissors

PROCEDURE
1. Tear the garbage bag down the sides so it is one large sheet.
2. Find a location where you expect to find animal activity, preferably a flat area away from pet and human traffic. Lay down the garbage bag and secure it with large rocks at the corners.
3. Carry the bucket of mud to the location and spread the mud over the garbage bag so it is about 1 inch (2.5 cm) thick. Test your mud's wetness by placing your hand on top. If your handprint is visible, you're good to go. If it disappears, your mud is too wet; if there is no handprint, it is too dry. (*See Figure 2*)
4. Put your attractant—peanut butter, birdseed, or food scraps—in the shallow tray and place the tray in the center of the mud. Leave it overnight. (*See Figure 3*)
5. Go to the location in the morning and check for tracks. Record your observations in your journal using the track ID guide to identify which animals visited your site.
6. Once finished, carefully cut through the plastic bag around the tracks and place it in a dry area to create a mold of each animal track you find. Clean the space; do not leave trays or garbage bags behind.

TAKE IT FURTHER
Move the track station to a new area or use different food to bait animals. During the winter, check tracks in the snow to determine which animals are also active!

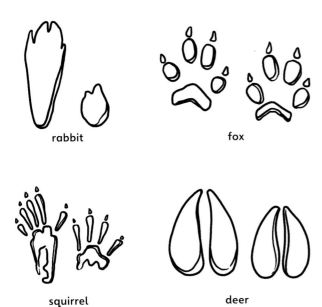

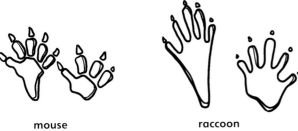
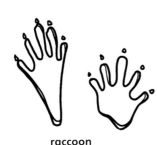

rabbit

fox

squirrel

deer

mouse

raccoon

Figure 1: Track ID guide

Figure 2: Spread the mud evenly over the bag.

Figure 3: Add the attractant in the center of the track plot.

NOW, THIS IS WILD!

Wolf tracks are one of the most prominent signs of their presence. Scientists track wolf packs to keep tabs on their whereabouts to reduce conflicts with humans, particularly for ranchers and farmers. They use plaster casts of wolf tracks that help identify specific members within the pack, contributing to the management of these magnificent creatures!

EXPLORE THE SCIENCE

Track stations are areas where scientists collect data by recording animal tracks and activity. These stations are beneficial when scientists want to observe the behavior of a specific species. Types include track plots, measured areas covered in sand or chalk at the bases of dens or travel routes, and track plates, such as the mud-covered one in this activity, with an attractant that can be placed anywhere.

TADPOLE PLAYGROUND

Tadpoles go through a fantastic metamorphosis to become adult frogs. In this activity, you will provide a safe and natural habitat for tadpoles to grow and thrive while you observe all the stages of their development.

ESSENTIAL QUESTION
Can you create a habitat that supports the growth and development of tadpoles into adult frogs?

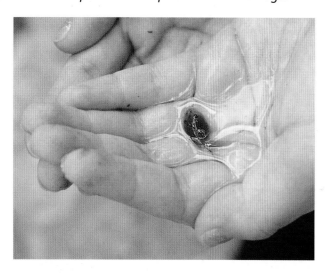

DIFFICULTY LEVEL: **Advanced**
SAFETY: 🐾

MATERIALS
- Small shovel
- Recycled shallow plastic container or tray that can hold water
- 2 gallons (7.5 liters) of rainwater (or tap water that has sat for a couple of days to remove chlorine)
- Rocks of different sizes
- Broken flowerpots
- Aquatic plants from a nearby pond (optional)
- Frog eggs from a nearby water source (optional)

PROCEDURE
1. Make sure you're near a lake or pond for this project. Find a location for the tadpole playground, preferably in a shady area with soil, like a garden. Frogs frequently burrow in the soil, so to ensure more success, do not place your playground near hard surfaces like pavement or concrete.
2. Use a small shovel to dig a hole and place the container inside so the top of your container is level with the ground. Not all frogs are great climbers, so being able to hop into your homemade pond is essential.
3. Fill the container with the rainwater. Never add water directly from the tap because it has been treated with substances that may be harmful to frogs.
4. Add rocks of different sizes to the container to provide shallow and deep areas for your frogs. Frogs can use the rocks to climb out of the water when needed. (*See Figure 1*)
5. Use the broken flowerpots to create shelters around the water source. This provides safety from both the sun and predators. Put soil and plants around and on top of the planters to help with camouflage.
6. Add aquatic plants, like duckweed, to help tadpoles and froglets hide.
7. You can either wait a couple of weeks for some frogs to find your area and lay eggs, or you can collect eggs from a nearby water source and add it to your setup. (*See Figure 2*) Do NOT purchase tadpoles and add them to your environment, as this may harm local frogs.

Figure 1: Set up your pond with rocks and plants.

Figure 2: Add frog eggs or tadpoles to your pond.

8. If leaves, bird droppings, or dead insects fall into the water, leave them there. They will act as a natural fertilizer. Add more rainwater as necessary.

9. Once eggs hatch, watch as they grow through their life stages over the next 14 weeks: tadpole, tadpole without gills, tadpole with legs, froglet, and adult frog—record your drawings and observations in your journal. Release your frogs where you found your frog eggs, if necessary.

TAKE IT FURTHER

Research local frogs in your area and learn more about their habitats. See if you can encourage a specific species to live in your constructed habitat by adding natural resources used by that species.

EXPLORE THE SCIENCE

Frog metamorphosis is a remarkable process with distinct stages of development. Fertilized eggs hatch into tadpoles with long tails and no legs—they are entirely aquatic and breathe through gills for the first four weeks. During the next four weeks, legs develop and the tail shrinks. In the following four weeks, the tail has nearly disappeared, both pairs of legs are fully formed, and the little froglet has adapted nicely to life on land, still spending some time in the water. Around the twelfth week, the frog is considered an adult, fully equipped for life on land with strong legs and lungs for breathing air.

NOW, THIS IS WILD!

Darwin's frog, a nearly extinct amphibian found in South America, takes fatherhood to the extreme! When fertilized eggs are close to hatching, the male Darwin's frog ingests the eggs and deposits them into his vocal pouch, where they hatch into tadpoles after three days. The tadpoles develop in their father's vocal pouch for six to seven weeks until they are froglets. Then the male expels the tadpoles into a water source to complete metamorphosis.

UNIT 2
ANIMAL DIVERSITY

Did you know there are approximately 1 to 2 million animal species on our planet? Surprisingly, 80 percent of land and 90 percent of sea species remain undiscovered! In this unit, you'll explore animal behavior as an ethologist, observing natural patterns. Design a Tweet Retreat to learn about our feathered friends. Challenge your detective skills in Poo's Clues, identifying animals by their scat. Witness earthworms making surprising choices in Squirmy Decisions. Catch some sneaky bugs in the Potato Pitfall, a clever trap designed for some up-close observations. Grab that notebook and embark on a journey of discoveries in the world of animals!

TWEET RETREAT

Become a birder by creating a birdwatching station to attract various bird species and observing their behavior. Using multiple platform bird feeders with different food sources, you will get a closer look at feathered friends right in your backyard.

ESSENTIAL QUESTION

Can you design and build bird feeders that attract a variety of bird species to your watching station?

DIFFICULTY LEVEL: **Moderate**
SAFETY: ✂ 🐾 🔥

MATERIALS

- Large craft sticks
- Hot glue gun with glue sticks, or wood glue
- Scissors
- Heavy string or twine
- Birdseed
- Fruit, cereal, or dried breadcrumbs
- Binoculars (optional)
- Bird ID books (optional)

PROCEDURE

I. Create the bottom of your platform feeder by placing six craft sticks next to each other. To secure the base, glue two craft sticks across the top and bottom of the six sticks.

2. Start building the walls by gluing two sticks on opposite sides of the base. They should be glued over stick no. I and stick no. 6 of your base. (*See Figure I*)

3. Take two sticks, and now glue over the sticks in the opposite direction.

4. Continue adding six to eight layers by adding two sticks, each layer in an opposite direction.

5. Cut four equal-length pieces of string and tie them around each corner of your feeder. (*See Figure 2*)

6. Find a window that overlooks a perfect place to set up a birdwatching station. This way, you can sit and observe during all seasons.

7. Fill your feeder with birdseed and hang it where you can see it from your window.

8. Make two more feeders that same way. Add fruit, cereal, dried breadcrumbs, or different kinds of birdseed to attract other birds to your station. You can use a pair of binoculars and bird ID books to identify the types of birds that visit your feeder.

TAKE IT FURTHER

Create other types of feeders using recycled materials around your home. For example, hang empty toilet paper rolls smeared with peanut butter and birdseed to create a buffet feeder. Or clean and decorate an empty milk jug to create a large feeder for hungry feathered friends.

Figure I: Glue 2 sticks to the base to build a wall.

Figure 2: Add string to all 4 corners.

EXPLORE THE SCIENCE

Platform bird feeders cater to various bird species because they offer open, flat surfaces for birds to access food easily. Additionally, they can hold multiple foods, including seeds, grains, nuts, and even fruit. Platform feeders become crucial during winter, nourishing birds with limited access to natural resources. By offering diverse foods all season, your platform feeders will attract many species of birds!

NOW, THIS IS WILD!

Competitive birders compete in a yearly birdwatching event called "Big Day," where participants aim to identify as many bird species as possible within 24 hours. During a Big Day event, birders travel to various habitats, such as forests, wetlands, and coastal areas, to maximize the diversity of species they can encounter. The current world record stands at an astonishing 757 bird species!

POO'S CLUES

When you're hiking or exploring an outdoor area, one way to discover which animals have been active is to look for clues. One place to start is to look for animal poo, called scat. Scat can give you a lot of information if you know what to look for.

ESSENTIAL QUESTION

What can you learn about animals by looking at their scat?

DIFFICULTY LEVEL: **Easy**

SAFETY: 🐾

MATERIALS

- Scat ID guide (*See Figure 1*)
- Ruler
- Stick

PROCEDURE

1. Go on a nature walk in a local state park or wildlife refuge. Don't forget to invite family members, friends, or another grown-up!
2. Watch for animal droppings, usually left along territorial boundaries, on prominent features, and sometimes right in the middle of a path or clearing.
3. When you find scat, never touch it with your hands, because some animal poo can pass along parasites and diseases. Use the scat ID guide to help you determine which animal made it. You may need to use your ruler to help identify the scat. (*See Figure 2*)
4. Use a stick to examine the scat, looking for signs of the animal's diet. Clues could be berries, bark, insects, fur, or bones.
5. Continue along your hike, identifying scat and recording observations in your journal.

TAKE IT FURTHER

Wintertime is an excellent time to look for scat because it's easier to see against snow and bare ground. Some wildlife have a different diet during winter, such as berries and flowers. Use your data to compare the scat of animals you have already identified in the area.

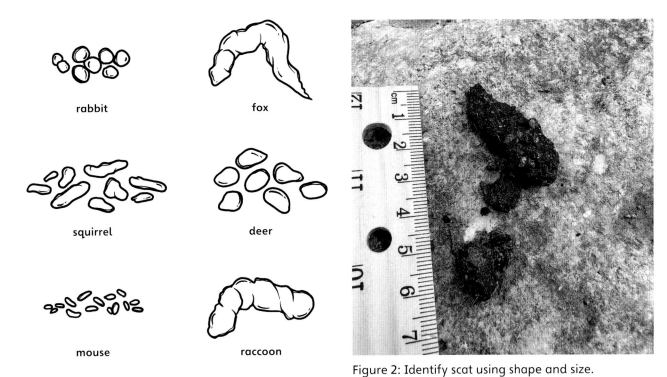

rabbit

fox

squirrel

deer

mouse

raccoon

Figure 1: Scat ID guide

Figure 2: Identify scat using shape and size.

NOW, THIS IS WILD!

Wombats are the only known animal that makes square poop! Wombats leave nearly 100 cube-shaped droppings on rocks, logs, or other elevated places to make their territory more visible. This extraordinary adaptation allows wombat scat to stay in place, marking their territory effectively and preventing it from rolling away.

EXPLORE THE SCIENCE

Identifying animals by their scat is crucial for wildlife tracking and research. Scat provides valuable information about species' presence, diet, behavior, and health. Researchers can also identify different species by distinct scat characteristics, helping to determine populations in an area. Scat provides a noninvasive method to understanding an animal's ecological role and impact on its environment.

SQUIRMY DECISIONS

Earthworms are found in one place—the dirt. So, if you give earthworms a choice of different environments, like ones with light, dry land, and smooth surfaces, how will they choose?

ESSENTIAL QUESTION
How do earthworms respond to different environmental conditions?

DIFFICULTY LEVEL: **Moderate**
SAFETY: 🐾

Note: Use the water dropper to keep the earthworms moist. Always handle the worms gently and with wet hands.

MATERIALS
- Paper towels
- Warm water
- Container with a lid, or a shoebox
- 2–3 earthworms
- Cardboard
- Stopwatch
- Flashlight
- Sandpaper

PROCEDURE
Test the following three environments.

Moist or Dry
1. Fold a dry paper towel and line half of a container. Wet another paper towel with warm water, fold it, and lay it down to line the other half. Be sure not to let the towels touch so the dry one doesn't absorb water from the wet one. (*See Figure 1*)
2. Place the earthworms in the center of the container so that half their body is on the moist paper towel and the other half is on the dry one. Cover the entire container with cardboard. Using your stopwatch, wait 5 to 10 minutes, then remove the cover and record your observations.

Light or Dark
1. Line the entire inner surface of the container with a moist paper towel.
2. Place a cover over half of the container. (*See Figure 2*)
3. Shine a flashlight onto the other half.
4. Place the earthworms in the center of the container so that half of their body is exposed to the light from the flashlight and the other half is under the cardboard. Wait 5 to 10 minutes, then remove the cover and record your observations. (*See Figure 3*)

Rough or Smooth
1. Dry the container and line half the inside with sandpaper.
2. Place the earthworms in the center of the container so that half of their body is resting

Figure 1: Add a wet and dry paper towel for the worm to choose.

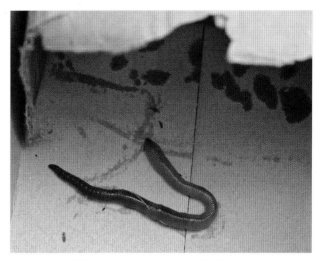

Figure 2: Add a cover to provide a dark side.

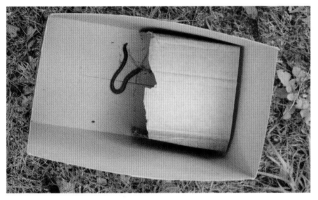

Figure 3: Always place the worms in the center of the choice box.

EXPLORE THE SCIENCE

Earthworms, vital for soil health, live in soil and breathe through their moist skin because they don't have lungs. Earthworms require moist environments to avoid drying out and prefer the darkness to avoid sunlight exposure. If you look closely, earthworms have tiny bristles called setae that help them navigate more easily on rough surfaces versus smooth surfaces, which can be slippery and challenging.

on the sandpaper and the other half is sitting on the container. (*See Figure 3*) Completely cover the container with cardboard. Wait 5 to 10 minutes, then remove the cover and record your observations.

TAKE IT FURTHER

What other environmental factors could you test? Try temperature, soil types, odors, different-colored light, or even vibrations!

NOW, THIS IS
WILD!

Microchaetus rappi, also known as the African giant earthworm, holds the impressive title of one of the world's largest earthworm species! These worms can grow to astonishing lengths, with the largest recorded in 1967, measuring 21 feet (6.7 m) in length and 0.8 inch (20 mm) in diameter!

31

8

POTATO PITFALL

Imagine a clever trap that can catch creatures as they walk by. The potato pitfall is such a trap, designed to capture insects, bugs, and other invertebrates, like slugs and snails, that live in or on the ground.

ESSENTIAL QUESTION

How can we observe tiny creatures like bugs and insects that live in or on the ground?

DIFFICULTY LEVEL: **Moderate**
SAFETY: ✂ 🐾

MATERIALS
- Large potato
- Knife
- Spoon
- Potato peeler
- Small shovel

PROCEDURE

1. With the help of a grown-up, carefully cut the potato in half lengthwise.
2. Use the spoon to scoop out the center of each half of the potato.
3. Carefully bore a hole into one side of the potato using either the tip of the potato peeler or a knife. This will be the entrance of the trap. (*See Figure 1*)
4. Place the potato halves back together.
5. Choose a location for your trap. Look for places where many critters could hide, like dead wood, shrubs, and flowers. Areas like the middle of your lawn won't produce the best results.
6. Use your small shovel to dig a shallow hole and place the potato inside. Cover with dirt.
7. Now, the hard part—because many insects and invertebrates come out at night, you'll need to wait 24 hours. But that doesn't mean you can't peek every once in a while!
8. Quietly uncover your potato and lift the top half off the next day. Observe and record all the animals you see in your trap. (*See Figure 2*) When done, cover the trap back up. Continue to check back daily, but you can also leave the potato in the ground as a tasty snack for critters.

TAKE IT FURTHER

Try different fruits and vegetables as pitfall traps. Would a soft and fleshy zucchini produce the same results, or perhaps a stringy pumpkin, or sweet, juicy watermelon?

Figure 1: Scoop out potato halves and add a hole to one side.

Figure 2: Remove the top and observe what fell into the trap.

EXPLORE THE SCIENCE

Entomologists studying arthropods, especially insects, will head into the field and collect them to understand their habitats. Scientists sometimes use a pitfall trap to collect and trap different insects. The most basic form is using a cup or a container buried in the soil and partially filled with a preservative to collect an insect to study. However, in our activity, we just want to observe, so our trap is a tasty treat that allows us to see various animals in the habitat, like pill bugs, millipedes, spiders, worms, and slugs.

In 2012, entomologist Michael Skvarla was heading into a Walmart to shop when an insect on the side of the building caught his eye. He captured it in a jar, took it home for his collection, and eventually forgot about it. Eight years later when he returned to his research, he made the startling realization that it was a rare giant lacewing, an insect that scientists thought was extinct in North America. These nocturnal beauties date back to the Jurassic Era more than 100 million years ago!

NOW, THIS IS WILD!

33

UNIT 3
ARTHROPODS

For all you budding entomologists, this exciting unit dives into the incredible world of arthropods, which make up a whopping 75 percent of all Earth's creatures. These jointed-legged critters are crucial in keeping our planet balanced, from pollination to nutrient recycling and serving as prey. Explore your backyard for spiders, ants, and centipedes. Find abandoned webs and preserve a spider's masterpiece in Web Wonders. Embark on a scavenger hunt, discovering the fantastic protective adaptations found in An Arthropod's Armory. Host some moths and butterflies for a Gooey Gathering using a secret recipe. Experience the secret glow some arthropods give off under UV light in Fascinating and Fluorescent. Don't let things bug you—get outside and check out the world of creepy crawlies!

9

WEB WONDERS

Explore the artistry and engineering of nature's greatest web designers—the orb weaver spiders. Many orb weavers build a new web every night, leaving old ones abandoned. So, step outside, being sure not to walk into a web, and check out the remarkable structures built by your eight-legged neighbors.

ESSENTIAL QUESTION

What can you discover about an orb weaver spider's behavior and web structure by collecting and observing its abandoned webs?

DIFFICULTY LEVEL: **Moderate**
SAFETY:

MATERIALS

- An empty spiderweb
- Talcum powder
- Black construction paper
- Hairspray

PROCEDURE

1. Search around for an abandoned orb spider web. To be sure no spider is home, gently tap on the border of the web. (*See Figure 1*) If there is a spider, the vibrations will make it come out to inspect.
2. Sprinkle talcum powder over the empty web. The fine powder will stick to the spider silk, making it easier to see. (*See Figure 2*)
3. Spray hairspray over a piece of black construction paper. While it's still tacky, put the paper behind the web and pull forward so the web sticks. Go slowly to ensure that the anchor points of the web don't snap off too quickly and collapse the web. (*See Figure 3*)
4. Spray the collected web with more hairspray, then set aside to dry.
5. Frame your new piece of art created by one of nature's finest artists!

TAKE IT FURTHER

Search around your home or on a nature walk for different webs. Each web design enables other species of spiders to hunt for insects in various habitats. Different types of webs to look for include funnel, cobwebs, mesh, sheet, and triangle webs.

anchor point | hub | support thread

radial thread | spiral thread

Figure 1: Diagram parts of a web

Figure 2: Carefully sprinkle powder onto the web.

Figure 3: Move slowly to collect the web with paper.

EXPLORE THE SCIENCE

With thousands of different species, orb weaver spiders are found worldwide, except for the Arctic and Antarctica. They build a new web to catch prey each night, hanging their survival by a thread. Spiders' webs are delicate, transparent, sticky, and incredibly strong, enough to snag a flying insect zooming by at incredible speeds. Posing no threat to humans and pets, orb weaver spiders are beneficial by keeping the insect population around their webs low.

NOW, THIS IS WILD!

The web of Darwin's bark spider spins record-breaking webs that measure about as long as two school buses. These massive webs span 82 feet (25 m) and are made of silk that is 10 times stronger than Kevlar, a material used as protective clothing and body armor.

10. AN ARTHROPOD'S ARMORY

Arthropods protect themselves using awesome physical features like pincers and barbs, tactics like mimicry to imitate other creatures, camouflage to blend in, and stinky odors to escape predators. You can discover these defense strategies in action in this point-based scavenger hunt!

ESSENTIAL QUESTION

How many types of protection can you recognize being used by arthropods?

DIFFICULTY LEVEL: **Easy**
SAFETY:

MATERIALS
- Sweep net, or wire hangers, pillowcase, large stick, and duct tape
- Large white paper or sheet
- Collection jars with lids
- Paper and pencil

PROCEDURE

1. Head outdoors to a field or grassy area with your sweep net. If you don't have a sweep net, make one by bending two wire hangers into a circle shape with straight parts at each end. Put a pillowcase over the circle, securely taping it on. Attach it to a large stick with duct tape. (*See Figure 1*)
2. Make teams for a scavenger hunt. Use the sweep net or your exceptional searching skills to find arthropods that use different forms of protection. Collect arthropods that don't bite or sting. If you're not sure, leave it alone!
3. Bring collected arthropods back to the large sheet to observe and record points for your finds based on the following point system (*See Figure 2*):
    - Arthropods with pincers (1 point); stingers (1 point); barbs on legs (2 points); forewings, which are stiff wings protecting softer wings underneath (2 points); bright colors (2 points); mimicry (3 points); camouflage (3 points); secretes smelly odor (3 points); playing dead (3 points).
4. The team with the most points wins at the end of a set time! Remember to record your arthropods in your science journal!

TAKE IT FURTHER

Take this scavenger hunt to different locations or play during different seasons and compare the arthropods you find.

Figure 1: Use wire hangers, a pillowcase, stick, and tape to create a catch net.

Figure 2: Observe the arthropods.

EXPLORE THE SCIENCE

Arthropods, including insects, spiders, and centipedes, have developed strategies to protect themselves from predators. One strategy is mimicry, which is like wearing a disguise. For instance, hoverflies will mimic bees to deter predators. Others, like walking sticks, camouflage or blend in with their surroundings, while beetles have tough shells, and scorpions wield powerful pincers. These defenses aid survival in environments teeming with hungry predators.

NOW, THIS IS WILD!

While mimicry is a great way to protect themselves from being eaten, some arthropods use it to be the hunter instead of the hunted. In 1879, travel writer James Hingsley was fooled so much by a mantis's mimicry that he reported that he saw an orchid flower catch and feed upon live butterflies. Orchid mantises have evolved to almost perfectly mimic an orchid blossom to devour unsuspecting pollinators, so much so that researchers have found that they attract more pollinators than the actual flowers do.

39

A GOOEY GATHERING

Since the 1800s, entomologists have been attracting and studying moths using a fascinating technique called sugaring. Moths are naturally drawn to sugar substances, so using a unique (and smelly) mixture, you will see how many different moth species you can attract.

ESSENTIAL QUESTION

How can you observe and study nocturnal moth species in your area?

DIFFICULTY LEVEL: **Moderate**
SAFETY: ✚ 🐾

MATERIALS
- Very ripe banana (the riper, the better)
- 2 ounces (60 ml) apple cider vinegar
- ²⁄₃ cup (227 g) brown sugar
- Bowl
- Spoon
- Plastic wrap
- Wide paintbrush (unused)
- Flashlight
- Red plastic wrap or cellophane (optional)
- Butterfly and moth ID guide (optional)

PROCEDURE

1. Peel the banana and place it into the bowl. Use the spoon to mash the ripe banana into a paste.
2. Add the apple cider vinegar and brown sugar to the banana and mix until you have a paintlike consistency. (*See Figure 1*) If the mixture is too runny, add another banana.
3. Cover the bowl with plastic wrap and place in a warm area several hours before sunset.
4. Find some trees that would be easily accessible at night, like on the edge of the woods or near some flowering plants. Just make sure they're away from bright lights and busy areas.
5. Just before the sun sets, use the paintbrush to paint a coat of this gooey mixture in long, narrow streaks onto the bark of several trees. (*See Figure 2*) Tip: Entomologists have found that warm nights with little to no wind, just before or after a rain, work best.
6. Set your timer and check the trees every hour. (*See Figure 3*) When observing the moths, try not to shine the flashlight directly on them, or they'll fly away. If you can, wrap the flashlight with red plastic to dim the light. Draw and record your observations in your journal. You can use a butterfly and moth ID guide to help identify what you've caught.

TAKE IT FURTHER
Try this technique for several nights in a row to compare the results of visitors to the gooey snack. There are many different recipes used in "sugaring" for moths. Try other recipes with the help of a grown-up to see if you attract different species.

Figure I: Prepare your sugary mixture.

Figure 2: Paint the mixture on trees.

Figure 3: Observe the moths and butterflies that are attracted to the mixture.

EXPLORE THE SCIENCE

Sugaring is a technique used by entomologists to attract and study moths and butterflies because these bugs are attracted to sugary substances. Entomologists have found adding a solid smell enhances sugaring's effectiveness. This is why our sugar mixture contains brown sugar and other ingredients, such as vinegar. Moths play essential roles in ecosystems as pollinators and as part of food chains, so studying them helps gain insights into the nocturnal world.

NOW, THIS IS
WILD!

Some moths, like the Luna and Atlas moths, do not eat in the adult stage of their lives. They don't even have a mouth or digestive tract! During the adult stage, which lasts only a week, their sole purpose is to mate. The energy for this is made possible by the moths eating so voraciously during their caterpillar phase.

41

12

FASCINATING AND FLUORESCENT

This discovery activity takes you into two realms often overlooked in the wild—the first is darkness. Heading out after the sun sets is thrilling and often leads to pleasant surprises. The second realm can only be seen using ultraviolet (UV) light and opens up an entirely new window into the world of arthropods.

ESSENTIAL QUESTION

How many arthropods can you find that glow under a UV light?

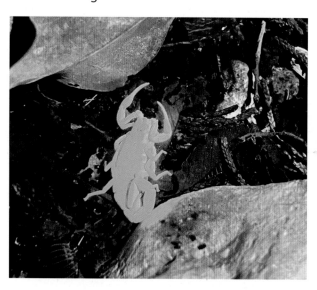

DIFFICULTY LEVEL: **Moderate**
SAFETY:

MATERIALS
- UV flashlight
- Red cellophane
- Gloves
- Collection cup

PROCEDURE

1. Prepare your flashlight by securing red cellophane around the light, preserving your night vision and not disturbing the organisms you are searching for. (*See Figure 1*)
2. Choose an area away from light to begin your search. Scanning the ground around rocks and bushes with UV light is an excellent place to start. You may need to pick up rocks and look under them. Next, look under leaves or on the bark of trees. Use your collection cup to observe what you find.
3. See if you can find any of the following arthropods that glow or have body parts that glow under a UV light (*See Figure 2*):
   - scorpion
   - centipede
   - millipede
   - firefly
   - some spiders (i.e., harvestman)
   - stick insects
   - some insect larvae
4. Release any arthropods you find, and record your findings in your journal.

TAKE IT FURTHER

Look for other animals or organic structures that glow under UV light, such as the silk fibers of a paper wasp nest, railroad worms, salamanders, and even some frogs!

Figure 1: Add red cellophane to your flashlight.

Figure 2: When you find an arthropod, check for a glow with the UV flashlight.

EXPLORE THE SCIENCE

The sun emits UV light or ultraviolet rays. Artificial sources like a UV flashlight can also emit UV radiation, causing fluorescence in some arthropods, like scorpions and millipedes, due to special chemicals in their exoskeletons. Scientists think this ability might help them communicate or regulate body temperature. Whatever the reason, they always look incredible!

NOW, THIS IS WILD!

The railroad worm, found throughout North and South America, is among a group of bugs that can glow under UV light. Unlike other bugs that shine yellow or green, this worm is the only insect that emits red light, making it stand out in the bug world!

UNIT 4
PLANTS

Budding botanists, welcome to the incredible world of plants! Plant diversity is astounding, ranging from tiny ground-hugging mosses to majestic towering redwoods and vibrant wildflowers that paint fields in a burst of colors. Plants have adapted to survive on land, a remarkable feat. Dive into the Mossy Masterpiece activity, where you'll become an artist creating living artwork that's sure to turn heads. Take a Sock Walk to find wild seeds and uncover the fascinating ways they spread and start new plants. Transform kitchen scraps into an outdoor garden in Scrappy Sprouts. Last but not least, witness the remarkable process of transpiration by leaves in Transpiring Tales. Get ready for a hands-on adventure that will cultivate a fresh appreciation for botany.

13

MOSSY MASTERPIECE

Moss's lack of roots and adaptability make it a perfect medium to create a living work of art. By arranging moss and other small natural items, you can create vibrant outdoor art pieces that could remain stunning with a bit of care.

ESSENTIAL QUESTION

Can you create a living masterpiece?

DIFFICULTY LEVEL: **Moderate**
SAFETY: 🌿

MATERIALS

- Chalk
- Piece of plywood, or flat surface in an indirect sun/shady location
- Sticks of different sizes
- Living moss (instructions for collection in the procedure)
- Old spatula or small shovel
- Natural items like small pebbles, pinecones, or leaves
- Nontoxic craft glue (optional)
- Water spray bottle or hose on mist

PROCEDURE

1. Use chalk to draw the first letter of your name on the plywood or flat surface in block lettering. Make sure it's large enough to add moss and materials for your art!
2. Arrange sticks and twigs along the outline. These sticks will act as the framework for your living moss art.
3. Collect moss from trees, sidewalks, or the forest floor (best after a rainfall) by sliding a spatula under moss to carefully lift it. (*See Figure I*) Don't grab it with your hands in clumps, as this will squish and destroy it. Be sure only to take some and leave over half where it is.
4. Place moss to fill in your framework, then get creative decorating with other natural items. Arrange them around the moss to add texture and style.
5. If you want to secure the moss and decorations more firmly, use the nontoxic craft glue to gently attach it to the plywood.
6. Regularly mist your living masterpiece to keep it moist. Avoid direct sunlight and overwatering. Now you and others can enjoy your work for a long time!

TAKE IT FURTHER

Use preserved moss that does not need watering and make another piece of art that can hang indoors for you to enjoy year-round!

Figure I: Use a spatula to carefully remove moss in large sections.

NOW, THIS IS WILD!

In 1997, scientists sent moss into space to see how it reacts without gravity. When they brought it back, they noticed something surprising: the moss was growing in a spiral, unlike any moss on Earth. No one knows precisely how plants sense gravity, but scientists think tiny particles called amyloplasts might be involved, and they're planning more experiments in space to find out. Maybe one day, you'll be part of the research team!

EXPLORE THE SCIENCE

Moss does not have traditional roots but absorbs water and nutrients through its leaves and stems. Instead of roots, moss has short rootlike structures called rhizomes that help keep it anchored to rocks, bark, and other surfaces. In this art project, the moss is placed on plywood, so with moisture and indirect sunlight, it will start to grow and spread, creating a living piece of art.

47

14

SOCK WALK

Plants can't move independently, so they depend on different ways to spread their seeds to new places. This nature sock walk will have you collecting, dispersing, and hopefully even helping plants find a new location to grow!

ESSENTIAL QUESTION

How have seeds adapted to travel to find new places to grow?

DIFFICULTY LEVEL: **Moderate**
SAFETY:

MATERIALS
- Large pair of socks
- Empty egg carton
- Magnifying lens
- Forceps
- Paper cup
- Soil

PROCEDURE

1. Place large socks over your shoes, fuzzy side out, and take a walk.
2. On your walk, try to pick up seeds on your socks. Seeds can be dispersed in the following ways:
   - wind, like dandelions
   - flying, like maple tree seeds with wings
   - eaten by animals, like berries and acorns
   - falling and rolling away, like acorns or pinecones
   - stick to animal fur, like burrs
   - popping open with force, like bittercress and some grass seeds
3. When the walk is complete, carefully remove your socks and use the magnifying lens to observe all the seeds you collected. (*See Figure 1*) Record your observations in your journal.
4. Remove some seeds from your socks using forceps (*See Figure 2*) and add them to a cup with soil. (*See Figure 3*) Cover the seeds with soil, add water, and set in the sun.
5. After about a week, come back and see what has sprouted!

TAKE IT FURTHER

Take a sock walk during various times of the year to gather seeds. Note the types of seeds available during each season, documenting observations and notes in your science journal.

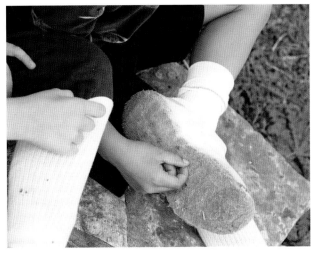

Figure 1: Check for seeds at the bottom of your socks.

Figure 2: Use forceps to carefully remove seeds.

Figure 3: Add seeds to a container to observe.

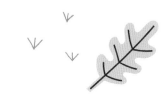

NOW, THIS IS WILD!

Giant sequoias are the largest trees on Earth, growing for thousands of years. However, in order to make more sequoias, they need fire. Sequoia cones have adapted to only open up and drop their seeds in extreme heat, like that of a wildfire. Needing only a bare mineral soil, the cones are covered with ash, and seedlings will grow in the spring.

EXPLORE THE SCIENCE

Plants have evolved various dispersal methods to enhance the survival and success of their seeds. By using different dispersal methods for their seeds, they reduce competition for resources like sunlight, water, and nutrients. Strategies such as wind, water, expulsion, and even animals help seeds find suitable environments to grow, ensuring the continuation of plant species.

15

SCRAPPY SPROUTS

Some people consider ordinary vegetable scraps a waste, but wait until you see what you can grow from them. In this activity, you will learn about plant propagation, turning waste into wonder.

ESSENTIAL QUESTION

How can vegetable scraps regrow into new plants?

DIFFICULTY LEVEL: **Easy**

SAFETY: ✂ 🌿

MATERIALS

- Various vegetable scraps (carrots, lettuce, onions, beets, ginger, garlic cloves, radish, celery, etc.)
- Scissors or knife
- Small containers or jars
- Water
- Soil
- Pots

PROCEDURE

1. Gather different vegetable scraps and cut them to preserve the part that can regrow (e.g., the carrot top, the base of lettuce, onion bottoms with roots, etc.).
2. Place the scraps in individual containers with enough water to cover the bottom part without submerging the entire scrap. (*See Figure I*)
3. Place on a sunny windowsill and continue to change out the water to keep it fresh and clean.
4. Once significant growth occurs, such as roots growing or visible sprouting, transfer the scraps to pots filled with soil, ensuring the roots are covered.
5. Place pots in a sunny spot and water the scraps regularly. Record their growth and your observations in your science journal.

TAKE IT FURTHER

Try different methods of propagation, such as with herbs. Take cuttings from healthy stems, remove the lower leaves, and place them in water. Roots will develop, and a new plant will grow from the cutting.

Figure I: Add scraps to water bowls until roots or sprouts form.

EXPLORE THE SCIENCE

Sprouts grow quickly because they contain all the essential nutrients needed for a plant to start to thrive. The plant will reabsorb the nutrients from the old plant into new root and leaf growth, which is the process of plant propagation. Propagation techniques are essential in science research, allowing us to learn about innovations in agriculture, biotechnology, and medicine.

A native Hawaiian plant species was declared extinct in the wild on Kaho'olawe island in 2015, but it has now found new life thanks to seeds collected from them before they died due to climate change. Researchers were able to grow the seedlings and then produce rooted cuttings, resulting in 23 new plants from propagation!

NOW, THIS IS
WILD!

16

TRANSPIRING TALES

Plants use a natural process called transpiration to release water vapor into the air. Water vapor moves from the plant to the air through tiny openings, called stomata, in their leaves. In this experiment, you'll investigate transpiration up close and discover how plants interact with their surroundings.

ESSENTIAL QUESTION

How does transpiration contribute to the water cycle and influence our environment?

DIFFICULTY LEVEL: **Easy**

SAFETY: ✂ 🌿

MATERIALS

- Various plants
- 3 large plastic baggies
- Duct tape
- Scissors

PROCEDURE

1. Choose three different plants, like a tree with large leaves, a tree with needles, and a plant with flowers.
2. Place a large plastic baggie over a few leaves of each plant, being careful not to rip the leaves.
3. Close the baggies as much as possible, then use duct tape to secure the baggie around the stem, covering any final places where air may escape. (*See Figure 1*)
4. Wait 20 to 30 minutes, then check the baggies. (*See Figure 2*) Record your observations in your journal.

TAKE IT FURTHER

Experiment at different times of the day to see if the transpiration rate varies based on the plant. Collect data over extended periods or during different seasons to see if transpiration rates vary with environmental conditions.

Figure I: Secure baggies around plants with tape.

Figure 2: Check baggies for evidence of transpiration.

NOW, THIS IS WILD!

Water transpired from a single tree has a cooling effect equal to two air conditioners in your home! When the atmosphere starts heating up, plants often release excess water from their leaves into the air. By releasing this evaporated water, plants also cool themselves and the surrounding environment.

EXPLORE THE SCIENCE

Transpiration, essential to the water cycle, circulates water through the environment. Plants absorb water from the soil, which travels up the stem and exits through leaf pores. Released water vapor contributes to the humidity and moisture of the surrounding atmosphere. Comparing transpiration observations across plants offers insight into how different types of plants and environmental conditions influence the rate of transpiration.

UNIT 5
TRAITS AND ADAPTATIONS

Welcome, biologists, to a world of survival secrets! Every living organism possesses adaptations—traits that help them survive and thrive in their environment. Adaptations are like custom-made gear for each living thing, significantly helping them excel in their habitat. Explore leaf diversity in Leave a Good Impression. Make an Everlasting Wish by understanding dandelion seeds. In Brilliant Beaks, learn how adaptations allow birds to tackle different food challenges in style. Then, gear up for a game of Camouflage 'n Seek, where you'll witness how nature's disguises can help you be victorious in this challenge.

17. LEAVE A GOOD IMPRESSION

Capture the intricate details and variations of leaves in this STEAM-inspired activity. Working with clay will allow you to observe unique sizes, shapes, textures, vein patterns, and the incredible diversity and beauty of leaves.

ESSENTIAL QUESTION

How do leaves share common traits while displaying unique differences among plant species?

DIFFICULTY LEVEL: **Moderate**

SAFETY: 🌿

MATERIALS
- Assortment of leaves
- Pencil
- Plastic wrap
- Cardboard
- Air-dry clay
- Rolling pin or large jar
- Plastic knife
- Bowl (optional)
- Acrylic paint and paintbrush (optional)

PROCEDURE

1. Gather as many different leaves as possible. Note their sizes, shapes, edges, textures, and vein patterns.
2. Use a pencil to take leaf rubbings in your science journal and make notes about what you see.
3. Cover a piece of cardboard in plastic wrap. Place the clay on top, then use the rolling pin to roll out the clay about ½ inch (1 cm) thick.
4. Place leaves vein side down onto the clay and gently roll over them into the clay.
5. Use a plastic knife to carefully cut around the leaf, keeping the edges as natural as possible. When done, carefully remove the leaf to reveal its impression. (*See Figure 1*)
6. Lift the plastic wrap gently. Place the clay leaf in a safe place to dry flat or in a plastic-lined bowl to get a curved shape.
7. Keep the natural clay color, or use acrylic paint to brighten up your leaf impressions.

TAKE IT FURTHER

Use the leaves and paint to make brilliant mandala art, create picture scenes using different size leaves, or develop a new artistic way to showcase the variety and beauty of leaves.

Figure 1: Gently remove leaves from the clay.

EXPLORE THE SCIENCE

Leaves vary widely in size, shape, and color and are one of the most essential parts of a plant because they capture sunlight energy for photosynthesis, a process that helps make food for plants. Inside the leaves are a network of veins that carry water and nutrients to the leaves. The veins also support the leaves, allowing the entire surface to get sunlight.

NOW, THIS IS WILD!

Victoria boliviana, a new species of colossal water lily, was identified in 2022 after it had been mistaken for another species for 177 years. *V. boliviana* is the world's largest waterlily species, with massive leaves that grow up to 10 feet (3 m) wide and can support a 175-pound (80-kg) adult!

57

18

EVERLASTING WISH

Capture the beauty of nature, possibly even a wish, by freezing a dandelion in a specific stage of its life cycle and dive into the science of why this is possible.

ESSENTIAL QUESTION

How does preserving a dandelion highlight its adaptation for seed dispersal?

DIFFICULTY LEVEL: **Easy**

SAFETY: ✂ ✚ 🌿

MATERIALS

- Dandelions
- Clean glass jar with a lid
- Wire cutters
- Copper wire
- Play dough, or air-dry clay

PROCEDURE

1. Find a patch of dandelions and pick the ones that have finished blooming and are about to open again. Look for the white tops. (*See Figure 1*)
2. Cut your dandelion stem(s) to fit inside your glass jar.
3. Cut your copper wire 1 to 2 inches (2.5–5 cm) longer than your stem. Slide the wire through the hollow stem until it reaches the head of the dandelion. (*See Figure 2*)
4. On the inside of the jar lid, secure the excess copper wire using a quarter-sized piece of clay. Adjust stems as needed.
5. Place the glass jar over the dandelions and secure it to the lid. Be sure that the dandelions are not touching the side of the glass jar.
6. Place the jar in a spot where it will not be disturbed, and in 24 hours, your dandelions will be frozen in time as long as they are protected from wind and movement!

TAKE IT FURTHER

Use other plants to make an everlasting display that features plants with only wind-dispersed seeds, such as catkins and pussy willows.

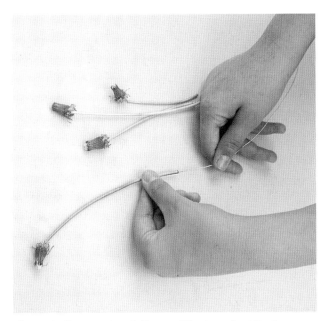

Figure I: Choose dandelions with closed white tops.

Figure 2: Slide the copper wire into the hollow stem.

NOW, THIS IS
WILD!

Dandelions are masters of survival and have been known to live up to I3 years if left untouched! With seeds traveling up to 3 miles (5 km), dandelions have been found to have roots I3 feet (4 m) long and have even taken root in gravel and cement!

EXPLORE THE SCIENCE
Dandelions solely depend on wind to disperse their seeds. Each seed bears a pappus, a group of feathery bristles that function as a parachute or sail to ensure they catch on the wind for dispersal.

19

BRILLIANT BEAKS

Birds exhibit various shapes and sizes, even in their beaks. This activity explores how varied beak shapes may give them advantages or disadvantages in acquiring food sources.

ESSENTIAL QUESTION

How do different bird beak shapes adapt to obtain various food sources?

DIFFICULTY LEVEL: **Moderate**
SAFETY: ✂ ✚

MATERIALS

- Scissors
- Paper
- Marker
- Bowl
- Cup of water
- "Food source" (natural items such as pebbles, acorns, and seeds; commercial items such as raw pasta, marshmallows, gummy worms, or rice)
- Paper plates
- "Beaks" (chopsticks, tweezers, slotted spoon, chip clip, eyedropper, etc.)
- Timer/watch

PROCEDURE

1. Cut a piece of paper into squares. On each square, use a marker to write a food source you are using. Try to have a minimum of five food sources, with one source being water in a narrow cup, which represents nectar. Fold up each piece of paper and place it in a bowl.

2. Place each food source on a paper plate at a place you designate as the "start." Place empty plates on the other side you set as the "finish." (*See Figure 1*)

3. Either by yourself or with some friends, choose one "beak."

4. Draw a paper from the bowl—this will be the food source that each bird "beak" will need to gather to bring to the "nest" (the plate at the finish line).

5. Start a timer and try to pick up as much food as possible using that "beak," then transport it to the "nest" in 30 seconds. When the timer stops, observe which "beak" most successfully transported that type of food.

6. Repeat steps 4 to 5 until all the "food" sources have been drawn. Record your observations in your science journal.

TAKE IT FURTHER

Observe birds in different habitats, such as forests, fresh water, grassy areas, etc. Notice how their beak shapes influence their survival, considering the availability of food sources. Make notes of beak sizes and shapes in your science journal.

Figure I: Start with plates of each type of food.

NOW, THIS IS
WILD!

The sword-billed hummingbird has the longest beak relative to its body size, sometimes even longer than its body, allowing it to feed on nectar other hummingbird species cannot. The bill is so long that this hummingbird must tilt its head upward to keep balance and use its feet to groom itself!

EXPLORE THE SCIENCE

Bird beak adaptations are crucial in reducing competition among different species in habitats. Birds evolved specialized beak shapes suited to specific food sources. When birds don't have to compete over food sources, each species evolves to find its niche or role, minimizing competition and maximizing the use of available resources.

20

CAMOUFLAGE 'N SEEK

Animals are hiding in plain sight all around you using camouflage. In this activity, you'll explore the art of blending in and the science behind it by creating your own camouflaged faces to play a twist on hide 'n seek.

ESSENTIAL QUESTION

How does camouflage help animals survive in their environments?

PROCEDURE

1. Collect natural materials that are small and lightweight.
2. Be creative and use the materials to make the face of an animal. Think about what good hiding spots would be outside, then glue the materials to the paper plates to make faces that can blend in with the environment.
3. Ask a friend or grown-up to play. Without them looking, hide your camouflaged paper plate faces. (*See Figure I*)
4. Have your friend or grown-up try to find the faces and notice how the camouflage adds a challenge to this classic game of hide 'n seek. Write about your observations in your science journal.

TAKE IT FURTHER

Consider how camouflage might change with the seasons. Would your animal hide as easily in the same spot during winter? Discuss how animals adapt their camouflage in winter versus summer.

DIFFICULTY LEVEL: **Easy**

SAFETY: **!**

MATERIALS

- Natural materials (leaves, pebbles, mulch, grass, etc.)
- 3–5 paper plates
- Glue

Figure I: Hide plates in an area using the camouflaged decorations.

EXPLORE THE SCIENCE

Camouflage is a survival strategy in which animals use color, patterns, and textures to blend into their surroundings, making them hard to spot. This adaptation helps them avoid predators or sneak up on prey, using their appearance to stay hidden and safe in their environment.

NOW, THIS IS
WILD!

One of the most venomous fish in the world is a master of camouflage—the stonefish. With I3 stout spines in the dorsal fin that can inject a highly toxic venom, they will sit perfectly still on the sea floor among rocks and coral until they ambush their unsuspecting prey, snagging it with their powerful jaws and swallowing it whole!

PART 2
EARTH SCIENCE

Earth Science is the study of planet Earth. It investigates the makeup of Earth, how the atmosphere determines weather and climate, the importance of the oceans that cover most of our planet, and Earth's role in the universe. Knowing Earth's materials, geological processes, and history helps scientists understand other planets—even those outside our solar system.

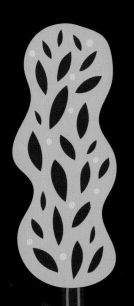

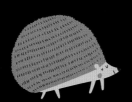

UNIT 6
ROCKS AND MINERALS

Prepare to uncover Earth's secrets as a young mineralogist studying rocks and minerals that narrate our planet's incredible story. Rocks are made of one or more minerals, which are naturally occurring, and are categorized by their properties, such as color, hardness, and crystal structure. In Rockhounds, you'll dive deep into the properties of both rocks and minerals while building a marvelous collection. Explore Cave Chemistry to understand stalagmite and stalactite formations. Use cold coffee dough to simulate fossil creation in Java Fossil Fun. Lastly, hunt for micrometeorites, a.k.a. space fragments, in Stardust Seekers.

21

ROCKHOUNDS

Each rock tells a story about where and how it was formed. In this activity, you'll find striking differences between rocks, just as you would for birds and trees, and hopefully start a fantastic collection.

ESSENTIAL QUESTION
What characteristics help identify rocks?

DIFFICULTY LEVEL: **Easy**
SAFETY: **!**

MATERIALS
- Field guide
- Egg carton

PROCEDURE
1. Decide where you would like to hunt for rocks and get permission from a grown-up. The best places to look for rocks are those with a mass of rock not covered by soil and vegetation, such as quarries (be sure to get permission), road cuts, outcrops, riverbanks, creek beds, and beaches.
2. Collect rock samples, looking for variations in texture, color, luster (shiny), density, foliations (layers), grain size, or lack thereof.
3. Once you have your rocks, begin by classifying them into three major groups: (*See Figure 1*)
   - **Igneous**—contains grains, or has no grains but appear glassy, and comes in many different colors; even grains are different colors.
   - **Sedimentary**—contains fragments of other rocks, like particles cemented together, has a range of grain sizes, will react to vinegar (tiny bubbles), and may contain fossils. Some have distinct parallel layers.
   - **Metamorphic**—shows bands or layers of different mineral grains, signs of bending or distortion, and grains appear flat.
4. Use your field guide to identify each rock specifically, label it, and place it in an egg carton to display your collection.

TAKE IT FURTHER
Imagine the travels of your rocks and write a story about their journey, imagining where they came from, how they formed, and what adventures they might have had throughout Earth's history.

Figure I: Use an egg carton to organize your rock collection.

NOW, THIS IS WILD!

EXPLORE THE SCIENCE

Rocks cycle continuously on Earth through three types: Igneous rocks are formed either underground (intrusive) from slowly cooling magma, or on the surface (extrusive) from quickly cooling lava. Sedimentary rocks are formed from layers of transported rock, compacting and cementing over time. Metamorphic rocks form when heat and pressure change existing rocks into magma, a significant step in the rock cycle.

In 2019, a giant raft of pumice the size of 20,000 football fields in the Pacific Ocean was spotted. This raft of floating rock formed after an underwater volcano erupted, and the frothy molten rock cooled. The raft drifted until it reached the Great Barrier Reef near Australia, bringing algae, barnacles, and coral to help replenish the endangered coral system.

22

CAVE CHEMISTRY

While formations in caves take millions of years to grow, try a sped-up version to grow "cave" crystals in just a few days.

ESSENTIAL QUESTION
Can you demonstrate the formation of stalagmites and stalactites?

DIFFICULTY LEVEL: **Moderate**

SAFETY: **!**

MATERIALS
- Epsom salt
- 2 small containers or jars
- Small stick
- Warm water
- 24-inch (60 cm) piece of cotton string
- 2 small rocks or washers
- Black construction paper

PROCEDURE
1. Pour Epsom salt into each container until full.
2. Add warm water to the top of each container. Stir while adding water to dissolve the salt.
3. Tie each end of the string to one of the small rocks or washers. This will keep the string on the bottom of the container.
4. Place the containers on either side of the paper. Add each rock with string to each container. Adjust the containers so that the middle of the string is about 1 inch (2.5 cm) above the paper. (*See Figure 1*)
5. Allow the containers to sit undisturbed for 3 to 5 days. Record your observations in your science journal.

TAKE IT FURTHER
Challenge yourself to see how large your stalagmite grows. Try adding food coloring to see if you can make your natural formations more colorful!

Figure 1: Adjust jars so the string is hanging just above the paper.

EXPLORE THE SCIENCE

Like this activity, stalagmites grow up from the ground in caves when water drips down through small cracks, leaving tiny bits of calcium carbonate behind when it evaporates. Stalactites hang down from the cave ceiling and form when water drips, leaving minerals behind. They build up over thousands of years, creating massive formations you can see today!

NOW, THIS IS
WILD!

The Giant Dome in Carlsbad Caverns National Park is the largest stalagmite ever discovered. Formed by mineral-bearing water dripping for 60 million years, this natural wonder looms at almost 62 feet (19 m)—that's as tall as a six-story building!

23

JAVA FOSSIL FUN

Brew up some fun when you remind your grown-ups not to let those morning coffee grounds go to waste. Turn them, along with a few simple ingredients, into fascinating mold fossils and unearth the secrets of the past!

ESSENTIAL QUESTION

Can you demonstrate the fossilization process by making mold fossils?

DIFFICULTY LEVEL: **Moderate**
SAFETY: **!**

MATERIALS
- I cup (80 g) used coffee grounds
- Natural objects
- ½ cup (120 ml) cold coffee
- I cup (125 g) flour
- ½ cup (144 g) salt
- Mixing bowl
- Wax paper

PROCEDURE

1. Ask a grown-up to save their coffee grounds and leftover coffee in the morning.
2. While the coffee cools, head out to collect natural objects like leaves, shells, seeds like acorns, or flowers.
3. Combine the coffee grounds, cold coffee, flour, and salt in a bowl until you have a doughlike consistency.
4. Divide the dough into equal parts. Roll each part into a ball, then flatten it onto wax paper using your hands.
5. Carefully press your natural objects firmly into the dough to leave an imprint. (*See Figure I*) Remove the object and leave your mold fossils to dry overnight.

TAKE IT FURTHER

Fill your dried fossil mold with white glue. This represents sediments accumulating in the impression over time. After 24 hours, gently pull the dried glue off. Now you have a cast fossil.

Figure I: Press natural objects into coffee dough.

EXPLORE THE SCIENCE

Mold fossils form when an organism's remains get buried in sediment, leaving an impression or "mold" in the rock after the remains decay. Later, if the mold gets filled with minerals from water or other sediment, it hardens into a cast fossil, preserving the shape and details of the original organism.

NOW, THIS IS WILD!

Two cattle farmers riding motorbikes on their property spotted massive black rocks. Upon further inspection, those "rocks" turned out to be the fossil remains of a new species of titanosaur, *Australotitan cooperensis*, estimated to weigh 70 tons (63 metric tons), stand two stories tall, and measure 98 feet (30 m) in length, about the size of a basketball court!

73

24

STARDUST SEEKERS

Every day, pieces of rock from space are broken up by Earth's atmosphere and rain down on us as dust. In this investigation, we dive into the world of micrometeorites to learn what they are, how to hunt for them, and how they made it to the surface of our planet.

ESSENTIAL QUESTION

What physical properties will show that we have found fragments of rocks from space?

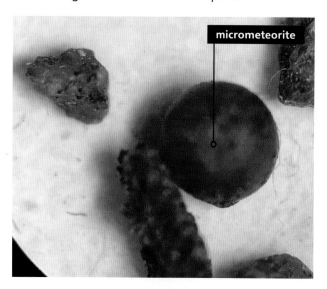

micrometeorite

DIFFICULTY LEVEL: **Moderate**
SAFETY: **!**

MATERIALS

- Deep tray (optional)
- Strong magnet (preferably neodymium)
- Plastic baggie
- White paper
- Magnifying lens or stereomicroscope
- Wooden skewer or sharp-tipped tool
- Sticky note or tape

PROCEDURE

1. Find a downspout around your home, then find the dirt and debris trail left behind after rain. Tip: If you can't immediately find a debris trail, place a deep tray under the downspout before the next rain. After it rains, pour the water from the tray, lay out the debris to dry, and move on to step 2.

2. Place the magnet inside a plastic baggie and run the protected magnet through the dirt and debris. (*See Figure 1*) Don't forget cracks in pavements and sneaky corners where dirt and debris hide!

3. Place the baggie with magnetized debris over a sheet of white paper, and slowly remove the magnet from the bag so everything falls onto the paper.

4. Use a magnifying lens or stereomicroscope to examine the debris. (*See Figure 2*) While most debris will not have a uniform shape, micrometeorites will be perfectly round and spherical. (*See Figure 3*) Tip: If you have a magnifying lens with two lenses of different sizes, the smaller one will generally have the higher magnification.

5. When you've found a micrometeorite, dip the end of a skewer in water and lightly touch the micrometeorite with the wet end. The micrometeorite will stick, and now you can transfer it to the sticky part of a sticky note to save your collection.

TAKE IT FURTHER

Micrometeorites fall as space dust every day on Earth. Try locations that may trap particles more easily, like a flat roof or a dried lake bed where the particles have settled.

Figure I: Use the magnet in the baggie to collect a sample.

Figure 2: Use a magnifying glass to start sorting through the sample.

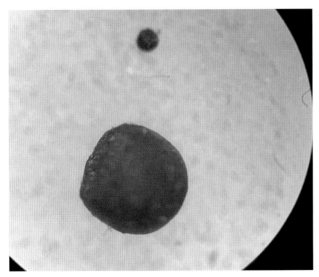

Figure 3: Identify micrometeorites, which are small, metallic, spherical shapes.

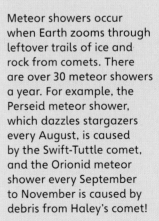

NOW, THIS IS WILD!

Meteor showers occur when Earth zooms through leftover trails of ice and rock from comets. There are over 30 meteor showers a year. For example, the Perseid meteor shower, which dazzles stargazers every August, is caused by the Swift-Tuttle comet, and the Orionid meteor shower every September to November is caused by debris from Haley's comet!

EXPLORE THE SCIENCE

Earth encounters space debris, primarily small bits of rock and metal, during its orbit. Upon entering Earth's atmosphere, they become meteors, burning up due to heat from friction. Surviving fragments land on Earth, now called meteorites, which can be rock, metal (nickel and iron), or both. Metallic meteorites are the easiest to find using a magnet. Smaller particles between 0.05 and 2 mm in diameter are called micrometeorites, characterized by their spherical shape from friction upon entering the atmosphere.

75

UNIT 7
EARTH'S CHANGING SURFACE

Embark on an adventure exploring Earth's dynamic transformations through weathering, erosion, and deposition, shaping landscapes over time. Don your geologist hat to study powerful forces that drive these processes. Become a soil engineer in Rooting for Stability, observing plants' foundation building. Witness the power of teamwork as you observe ants moving soil and benefitting other ecosystems in Soil Farmers. With Sweet Sinkholes, build a sinkhole model and discover how the ground beneath our feet can change instantly. Conclude with Core Sampling, uncovering hidden layers beneath the surface.

25

ROOTING FOR STABILITY

Sometimes, it can be hard to appreciate what we cannot see happening below the surface of the Earth. This investigation of roots helps you discover how nature's engineering of root systems prevents erosion.

ESSENTIAL QUESTION

How do different soil environments impact soil erosion?

DIFFICULTY LEVEL: **Advanced**
SAFETY: ✂ 🌿

MATERIALS

- 6 bottles with lids all the same size (water bottles, 2-liter soda bottles, or milk jugs)
- Marker
- Scissors
- Clay
- Bare soil
- Mulch and leaf litter
- Grass
- Hole punch
- Cotton string
- Water

PROCEDURE

1. With your marker, draw a large rectangle on the side of 3 bottles. Make sure the rectangles are the same size.
2. With the help of a grown-up, cut out the rectangles. (*See Figure 1*)
3. Place the bottles on a sturdy surface, undisturbed, with the open rectangles facing up—place clay on either side of the bottles to keep them from rolling.
4. Add the following:
   - Bottle 1: Bare soil
   - Bottle 2: Bare soil with mulch and leaf litter on top
   - Bottle 3: Soil with grass growing
5. Cut the top off the other three bottles and use the hole punch to make two holes across from each other on the cut side.
6. Cut three lengths of string about 8 inches (20 cm) and attach each to the cups at the holes, making handles.
7. Hang the collection bottles from the necks of the filtration bottles with soil. (*See Figure 2*) Remove caps from the filtration bottles.
8. Pour equal amounts of water into each filtration bottle until it flows into collection cups. Compare the water filtered through each soil environment and record observations in your science journal.

TAKE IT FURTHER

Analyze the water quality difference of samples collected, noting how erosion and runoff could lead to pesticides or other chemicals flowing into streams and lakes.

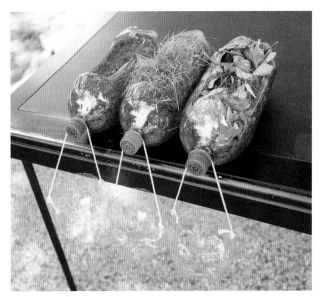

Figure 2: Hang collection bottles from the filtration systems.

Figure I: Cut rectangles into the soda bottles.

EXPLORE THE SCIENCE

Rooted plants are vital in preventing soil erosion by binding soil particles together with their roots. This helps the plants resist wind and water erosion forces. Mulch and leaf litter further prevent erosion by breaking the fall of water droplets, thereby decreasing the force that could dislodge soil particles. They also assist in moisture retention, preventing soil from becoming dry and prone to erosion.

NOW, THIS IS WILD!

Mangrove forests that grow along coastlines in tropical and subtropical regions have specialized roots that emerge from their trunks and extend above water and soil surfaces, making them a coastal defense against floods and tsunamis. This unique root system is a natural barrier that slows down waves, reducing shore erosion, trapping sediments, and helping build up land!

26

SOIL FARMERS

If you've ever worked in a group, you know the importance of teamwork, and no animal understands it better than ants! In this activity, you'll witness for yourself not only their incredible teamwork but also how their bustling habitat improves the ecosystems around them.

ESSENTIAL QUESTION
How do animals improve the health of soil?

DIFFICULTY LEVEL: **Advanced**
SAFETY: ✂ 🐾

MATERIALS
- Clear, wide-mouthed container with a lid
- Soil
- Marker
- Cotton ball moistened with water
- Small pieces of fruit
- Mesh material (old stocking or old screen)
- Long-handled spoon
- Scissors
- Black construction paper
- Tape

PROCEDURE
1. Fill a container with soil, leaving about 2 inches (5 cm) of room at the top. Mark the top of the soil level with the marker.
2. Place a moistened cotton ball and small pieces of fruit inside the container.
3. Measure and cut a piece of mesh material to fit over the opening of the container. Leave a little extra around the edges.
4. Poke several holes in the lid of the container and ensure it holds the mesh firmly on the container to prevent accidental escapees.
5. Locate an anthill. Ask an adult to help identify the ants that don't bite. Place your container near the anthill and use the long-handled spoon to scoop about 15–20 ants to place in your container. (*See Figure 1*)
6. Immediately cover your container with the mesh and lid. Observe your temporary pets until they settle down. Record your observations in your science journal.
7. Cut black construction paper to the size of your container and tape it on to make ants think they are underground.
8. Keep the ant farm in a quiet area with indirect light at room temperature and check on them several times a day for a week as they create tunnels and chambers. Note the soil level and record all observations in your science journal. (*See Figure 2*)
9. Add a cotton ball with water and small pieces of fruit as needed. After a week of observations, return ants to their colony.

TAKE IT FURTHER
Make several ant farms and connect them with clear tubing to observe the social nature of ants, noting how they move, communicate, and work.

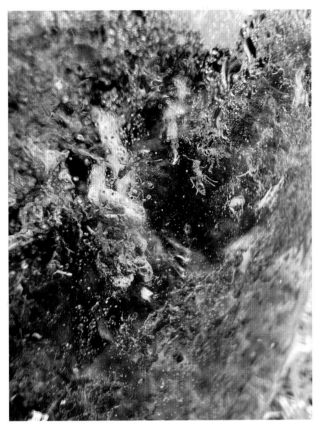

Figure 1: Collect ants from an anthill.

Figure 2: Check on the ants several times a day.

It is estimated that there are about 20 quadrillion ants on our planet, outnumbering humans 2.5 million to one. With so many ant colonies, one stands out as the largest on Earth—the Argentine Ant Supercolony, spanning more than 3,700 miles (5,900 km), hosts a massive population of 307 million ants!

NOW, THIS IS WILD!

EXPLORE THE SCIENCE

Ant farms allow us the opportunity to see the role ants play in soil formation and their importance in developing healthy soils. Ants move vast quantities of soil to the surface when constructing underground tunnels, burrows, and storage galleries. This soil is often high in carbon and nitrogen, vital nutrients for plant growth.

81

27

SWEET SINKHOLES

Sinkholes are naturally occurring depressions beneath the Earth's surface. Using everyday items, you can unravel the secrets of how sinkholes form and the geological processes that lead to them.

ESSENTIAL QUESTION

Can you create a model that shows the process of sinkhole formations?

DIFFICULTY LEVEL: **Moderate**
SAFETY: ✄

MATERIALS

- Scissors
- 16 oz (475 ml) Styrofoam cup
- Coffee filter
- Toilet paper roll
- Sugar
- Sand
- 2-liter soda bottle
- Water

PROCEDURE

1. Use scissors to create a quarter-sized hole in the bottom of the cup.
2. Place a coffee filter inside the cup, covering the bottom.
3. Place the toilet paper roll inside the cup and fill it with sugar. Fill around the outside of the toilet paper with sand. (*See Figure I*)
4. Carefully remove the toilet paper roll. Add a thin layer of sand over the sugar.
5. Cut the 2-liter soda bottle to the height of the Styrofoam cup and fill halfway with water.
6. Place the Styrofoam cup upright in the water. The water's surface (which models groundwater) should be level with your top layer of sand.
7. Observe as the top layer of sand sinks to avoid being left behind. Record your observations in your science journal.

TAKE IT FURTHER

Fill a glass dish with a mix of sugar cubes (representing limestone), rocks, and sand, and cover it with clay to create a landform. Make small cracks in the top and pour water, watching from the side how cave structures form over time.

Figure I: Add sugar inside the toilet paper roll and sand on the outside of the roll.

EXPLORE THE SCIENCE

Sinkholes form when limestone is gradually dissolved by groundwater, creating cavities beneath the surface. As the limestone dissolves, the ground above can collapse suddenly, especially after heavy rainfall or changes in water levels, resulting in a sinkhole. These sinkholes often reveal an underground cave system formed over millions of years of erosion of the rock below.

NOW, THIS IS
WILD!

Billionaire Johnny Morris opened a golf course in Missouri in 2014, but a massive sinkhole formed a year after. Morris was curious, so he hired a team to start digging and rediscovered an underground cave system 2,000 feet (600 m) below the surface. Morris is now building a resort overlooking this natural wonder!

28

CORE SAMPLING

DIFFICULTY LEVEL: **Moderate**
SAFETY: **!**

MATERIALS
- Different types of earth material (dry, hard-packed dirt, loose soil, gravel, silt, sand, clay, leaf litter)
- Ruler
- Clear cup or container
- Spray bottle filled with water
- Clear plastic straw
- Magnifying lens

Geologists love to explore the secrets hidden beneath the surface of the Earth, and one way they do this is by using a method called core sampling. By simulating the geological process of layering earth materials, you will investigate how these layers stack up over time.

ESSENTIAL QUESTION
How can core samples accurately picture what is below Earth's surface?

PROCEDURE
1. Choose one of the earth materials and use a ruler to add a ½-inch (1 cm) layer to the container.
2. Mist with the spray bottle until the dirt is damp but not soaked.
3. Place another layer of different dirt ½ inch (1 cm) deep on top of the first layer and moisten with the spray bottle until damp. (*See Figure 1*)
4. Continue to add three more layers of earth materials in any order you choose, moistening with water between each layer.
5. Push a straw straight down to the bottom of the cup. To extract a core sample, place your finger tightly over the top end of the straw and pull the straw out of the cup. (*See Figure 2*)
6. Observe the straw core sample layers using a magnifying lens and record observations in your science journal. Create several samples by changing the layers, then compare core samples.

Figure 1: Add layers to the container, being sure to spray in between.

Figure 2: Extract a sample from the container.

EXPLORE THE SCIENCE

Core sampling is a technique to collect samples of rock, soil, or ice from beneath the Earth's surface. Core samples help geologists examine layers to observe changes in sedimentation, identify fossil records, and determine properties of Earth's subsurfaces. This information aids in understanding past climates, geological events, and the overall history of Earth.

NOW, THIS IS WILD!

A team of scientists aboard the research vessel Neil Armstrong broke records in 2022 by collecting a 38-foot (11.5 m) long core sample from the deepest part of the Puerto Rico trench, nearly 5 miles (8 km) below the surface of the Atlantic Ocean. They brought up tons of data dating back to millions of years ago.

TAKE IT FURTHER

Explore your surroundings to observe natural rock or soil layers, such as road cuts and eroded landscapes. Make sketches and notes in your science journal, noting colors, fossils found, and types of rocks, and what they might reveal about the history of your local area.

UNIT 8
NATURAL RESOURCES

Unlock the incredible potential of our natural resources as an environmental engineer. These resources, found in nature, include sunlight, wind, water, and air. Craft a windsock in Wind Detector to understand wind patterns. Build a unique particle trap, exposing what may lurk in the air you breathe in Air's Dirty Secrets. Let your inner engineer come out with A Flora Fling where you'll build a slingshot to send out seed bombs of wildflowers. Use the sun's power to create unique art using Solar Etching. This adventure combines your scientist, engineer, and artist skills into one!

29

WIND DETECTOR

Some weather instruments don't need to be complex to observe weather patterns. In this activity, you'll build a strip-style windsock to track changes in wind direction and wind flow.

ESSENTIAL QUESTION

Can you build a windsock to track movements in the wind?

DIFFICULTY LEVEL: **Moderate**
SAFETY: ✂

MATERIALS

- Scissors
- 2-liter soda bottle
- Hole punch
- String
- Plastic tablecloth or plastic grocery bags

PROCEDURE

1. Cut a 2-inch (5 cm) ring from the soda bottle by carefully cutting off the top and bottom.
2. Use the hole punch to make two holes opposite each other in the plastic ring.
3. Cut about a 2-foot (60 cm) piece of string. Tie each end to the holes so you can now hang the windsock. (*See Figure 1*)
4. Cut eight strips from the tablecloth. Each strip should be 1 inch (2.5 cm) wide and 2 feet (60 cm) long.
5. To attach the plastic strips to your ring, fold them in half longways. Place the loop from the fold inside the ring, then bring the end of the strip around the outside of the ring through the loop. (*See Figure 2*) Pull ends through to secure the strip to the ring. Repeat with the other seven strips around the plastic ring, ensuring all loose ends point in the same direction.
6. Hang your windsock securely in a place where the wind blows unobstructed. Watch your windsock and record observations in your science journal.

TAKE IT FURTHER

Analyze the relationship between your windsock observations and the official wind data from weather data sources. Note any similarities or differences between your report and official conditions.

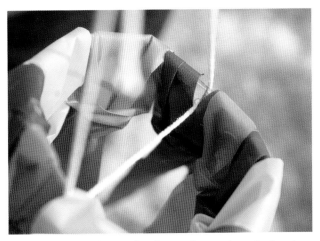

Figure 1: Add holes and string to hang the windsock.

Figure 2: Loop strips around the plastic ring.

EXPLORE THE SCIENCE

Windsocks are simple visual aids indicating wind direction. Blowing wind catches the windsock strips, extending and aligning them with the direction of the wind. Each strip independently responds to the wind direction, collectively indicating the wind flow pattern due to their flat shape and flexibility reacting quickly to gentle wind movements.

NOW, THIS IS WILD!

Commonwealth Bay, Antarctica, holds the record for being the windiest place on the planet. This area has catabolic winds, or winds that blow down a slope because of gravity, over 150 miles per hour (240 km/h) daily, sometimes reaching 200 mph (320 km/h)!

30

AIR'S DIRTY SECRETS

Do you ever wonder why you sneeze when you head outdoors or why the air sometimes looks a little dirty? Become an air quality detective to discover the cause and learn how to understand air quality.

ESSENTIAL QUESTION
How clean is the air you are breathing?

DIFFICULTY LEVEL: **Moderate**
SAFETY: ✂

MATERIALS
- Scissors
- Cardstock
- Ruler
- 1-inch (2.5 cm) hole punch or quarter
- String
- Clear packing tape
- Marker
- Magnifying glass

PROCEDURE
1. Cut three strips of cardstock 2 inches (5 cm) wide by 10 inches (25 cm) long.
2. Use the hole punch to make four or five circles in the strip. (If you don't have a hole punch, trace a quarter and cut out the holes.)
3. Punch a small hole in the top of the strip and tie a string through the hole.
4. Place a long strip of packing tape over one side, completely covering the holes. (*See Figure 1*) The other side will be sticky, so be careful not to touch it!
5. Determine the date and locations where you will hang the strips—note this information on the strip. Hang the strips and leave them undisturbed for 24 hours.
6. Collect the samples and view them with your magnifying lens. (*See Figure 2*) Can you determine if particles are from plants, insects, or dust? Record any observations about the types of particles you see, along with the weather conditions, date, and season.

TAKE IT FURTHER
Check a weather app and determine the day's Air Quality Index (AQI). The higher the AQI value, the greater the level of air pollution. Use this to determine how healthy the air quality is, then test again when the AQI is higher or lower. Compare your results. Can you come up with another way to collect particles?

Figure 1: Add tape to one side of the cardstock to create a particle trap.

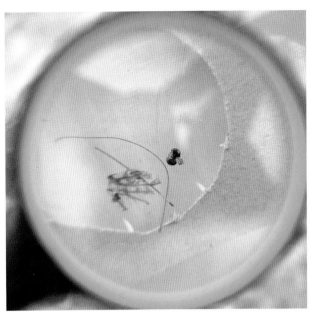

Figure 2: Use a magnifying glass to observe particles that were trapped.

EXPLORE THE SCIENCE

Air, primarily gas, contains solid and liquid particulates, causing particle pollution. Sources include vehicle exhaust, smokestacks, pollen, volcanic ash, dust, and wildfires. Particle pollution causes problems with humans' respiratory systems and contributes to smog and acid rain. Concentrations of particulates outdoors vary due to factors like season, weather, and wind.

NOW, THIS IS WILD!

In December 1952, a severe air pollution event known as the Great Smog of London lasted five days. Cold weather, windless conditions, and coal burning caused this event, leading to thousands of deaths. This prompted significant changes in air quality regulations.

31

A FLORA FLING

Discover how seed bombs can transform spaces into vibrant, blooming havens for local wildlife. Roll up your sleeves, craft some wildflower seed bombs, and sling these tiny parcels of life into the environment.

ESSENTIAL QUESTION

How can we support the growth of natural habitats and positively impact local ecosystems?

DIFFICULTY LEVEL: **Moderate**

SAFETY: ✂

MATERIALS

- Bowl
- 1 cup (115 g) potting soil or compost mixture
- ½ cup (63 g) flour
- Wildflower seeds native to your local ecosystem
- Water
- Egg carton or wax paper
- Uninflated balloon
- Scissors
- Toilet paper roll or paper tube
- Strong tape

PROCEDURE

Part 1: Seed Bombs

1. Mix the soil and flour thoroughly, then gently add seeds.
2. Add water one tablespoon (15 ml) at a time until the mixture feels like dough. If the mix gets too wet, add a little more soil.
3. Shape the mixture into small balls—larger than a marble but smaller than a table tennis ball.
4. Place balls into an egg carton or on wax paper overnight to dry. (*See Figure 1*)

Part 2: Slingshot

1. Tie a knot in your balloon to give you an excellent handhold to pull back your sling.
2. Cut the round top of your balloon off and wrap it around one end of your toilet paper roll. Secure with tape.
3. When the seeds bombs are dry, add one to your slingshot, pull back on the balloon, and launch the bomb into the area you want to seed with wildflowers. Slingshot the rest of your bombs in different areas. (*See Figure 2*)

TAKE IT FURTHER

Explore seed collecting by gathering seeds from mature wildflowers grown from seed bombs. Host a seed exchange where participants can trade seeds and learn about native species.

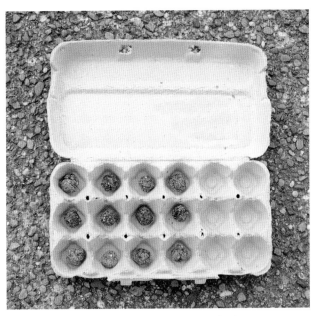

Figure I: Dry and store your seed bombs in an egg carton.

Figure 2: Use the slingshot to launch the seed bombs.

EXPLORE THE SCIENCE

Wildflowers are vital reservoirs of biodiversity, serving as habitats and nesting sites for bees, moths, butterflies, and other insects. The wildflowers also support a wide range of wildlife, including birds, bats, small mammals, and specific amphibians, showcasing the ecological importance of wildflowers as a foundational natural resource.

NOW, THIS IS WILD!

Like most seeds, wildflower seeds can lay dormant for years, even decades. But, when there is heavier than average precipitation during winter, along with warm, moist wind, a rare event occurs—a superbloom. Superblooms are the blooming of an above-average number of wildflowers that are so massive and colorful, they can be seen from space!

32

SOLAR ETCHING

Harness the power of sunlight using a magnifying glass to create unique designs on wood. In this activity, you'll explore how concentrated heat can be used to make intricate patterns.

ESSENTIAL QUESTION

How can sunlight be manipulated to create works of art?

DIFFICULTY LEVEL: **Advanced**
SAFETY: 🔥 👁

Note: Adult supervision may be necessary.

MATERIALS
- Clean pieces of wood
- Pencil
- Paper
- Magnifying lens, 4-inch (10 cm) diameter
- Protective eyewear (such as welding goggles)

PROCEDURE

1. Draw your design on the wood or make a rough draft using paper and pencil. If using paper, place the drawing on top of the wood and draw over your rough draft, pressing the pencil into the wood. Lift the paper and use a pencil to draw outlines to follow.

2. Place the wood in front of you with your back to the sun shining over the shoulder of your writing hand (if left-handed, sun over left shoulder; if right-handed, sun over right shoulder). Note that this activity will not work on an overcast or rainy day.

3. Put on protective eyewear.

4. Hold the magnifying glass above the wood, allowing the sunbeam to shine. To start burning the wood, you must see a perfect circle or a focal point. (*See Figure 1*) Try to get this focal point as small as possible. The circle will enlarge and stop burning if you get too close to the wood.

5. To create your design, move the focal point toward your pencil line, going back and forth. Move slowly along your sketch until it's complete. (*See Figure 2*) Be careful, as the beam is HOT! Never let the beam touch anything but the wood!

TAKE IT FURTHER
Make more intricate designs using different-sized magnifying glasses, and continue practicing to hone your craft of pyrography!

Figure 1: Use the magnifying glass to create a focal point.

Figure 2: Move slowly to be sure you've etched into the wood.

EXPLORE THE SCIENCE

Pyrography is the art of decorating wood or other materials with burn marks from controlled application of heated objects—in this case, the sun. Sunlight passing through a magnifying glass's convex lens converges at a focal point, creating a concentrated beam of light that ignites flammable material like wood.

Fresnel (pronounced "Fra-nel") lenses, invented in the 1820s to improve lighthouses to shine light farther and through dense layers of fog, are unique in that they have special ridges that can capture light and steer it in one direction, decreasing tragic and fatal shipwrecks that were prevalent in the 1800s.

NOW, THIS IS WILD!

UNIT 9
WEATHER AND CLIMATE

Breeze into a world of weather and climate as a young meteorologist! Study atmospheric rhythms, from short-term changes to long-term trends, like temperature, rainfall, and wind speed, to plan fun activities, make predictions, and stay safe during extreme weather. Build a rain gauge with the Rainy Day Tracker to measure seasonal showers. Use A Simple Nephoscope to record the clouds' direction and speed. Craft a barometer in Feeling the Pressure to get a reading on atmospheric changes. Wrap up the unit by discovering how clouds are created by making your own in Cloud Chamber.

33

RAINY DAY TRACKER

By creating and using a rain gauge in this activity, you will discover how this simple yet powerful tool helps scientists understand and track precipitation to predict patterns.

ESSENTIAL QUESTION

What patterns can we observe in rainfall measurements over a specific period?

DIFFICULTY LEVEL: **Easy**
SAFETY: ✂

MATERIALS
- 2-liter plastic bottle (label removed)
- Scissors
- Plastic metric ruler
- Duct tape
- Small pebbles
- Water
- Marker

PROCEDURE

1. Use scissors or ask a grown-up for help to cut the top section of the plastic bottle off carefully. Be sure the cut is straight across to create an open container.
2. Place the metric ruler vertically inside the bottle, ensuring it touches the bottom. (*See Figure 1*) Use duct tape to attach it securely. (If you don't have a ruler, tape duct tape inside, and use a measuring tape and a marker to mark every ¼ inch (½ cm).
3. Place pebbles and water in the bottom of the bottle to add weight to prevent it from tipping over. Mark the water level with a marker and begin gauging the rainfall from this measurement.
4. Place the top of the bottle upside down into the bottom to form a funnel. Secure the two halves together with tape. (*See Figure 2*)
5. Whenever it rains, measure the depth of the collected rainwater using the ruler attached inside. Record the data in your science journal, including the date and weather conditions.
6. After recording the rainfall, empty the gauge and reset it for future measurements.

TAKE IT FURTHER

Keep track of rainfall data over time to analyze trends and compare how your data matches local weather forecasts and news stations.

Figure 1: Place the ruler inside the bottle.

Figure 2: Create a funnel to help collect rainwater.

EXPLORE THE SCIENCE

Rain gauges measure rainfall in a specific area, providing valuable data for meteorologists, hydrologists, and climatologists. This data aids in understanding precipitation patterns, water management, and climate studies, identifying trends such as seasonal rainfall, drought patterns, or climate shifts.

NOW, THIS IS WILD!

Although cartoons and illustrations depict rain as a circle or a drop, rain with a radius over 1 millimeter has a shape more like that of a hamburger bun. When raindrops get larger than 4 millimeters, they distort into a shape like a parachute, eventually breaking into smaller drops.

99

34

A SIMPLE NEPHOSCOPE

Sometimes, it's tricky to tell which way the wind blows just by stepping outdoors. While some ground indicators could help us, today we're going to check indicators in the sky—clouds—to determine wind direction by building a simple tool called a nephoscope.

ESSENTIAL QUESTION

How can you determine the direction of the wind using clouds?

PROCEDURE

1. Head outside on a day with some wind and clouds in the sky.
2. Lay the mirror face up in a grassy area away from trees and buildings where you have a good reflection of the clouds.
3. Find North using your compass, then label the mirror edges with the cardinal directions (N, E, S, W) using a dry-erase marker. (*See Figure 1*)
4. Look at the cloud reflections and find one you see close to the mirror's edge. Mark the cloud reflection with an *X* to indicate that it will be the one you are tracking.
5. As the cloud moves across the mirror, plot its movement by marking it with a large dot.
6. Connect the dots of the cloud's movement on the mirror. (*See Figure 2*) This line indicates the wind direction, noting where the wind is coming from, as meteorologists do in their reports. Report your observations and findings in your science journal.

TAKE IT FURTHER

Compare the wind direction you found with the direction based on ground indicators, such as windsocks, wind vanes, or drifting smoke. If different, determine the reason.

DIFFICULTY LEVEL: **Easy**
SAFETY:

MATERIALS
- Old, framed mirror
- Compass
- Dry-erase marker

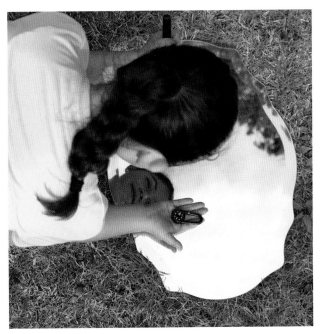

Figure I: Use a compass to identify cardinal directions on the mirror.

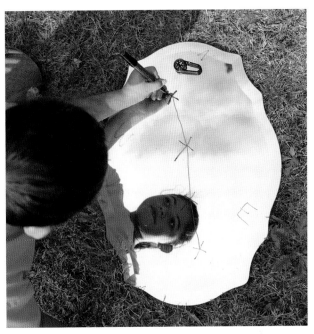

Figure 2: Connect your marks to track the movement of the clouds.

EXPLORE THE SCIENCE

A nephoscope tracks cloud movement using geometry and optics. Placing a mirror flat on a surface creates a clear reflection of the sky, aiding meteorologists in determining wind direction at various altitudes for accurate weather predictions. Especially useful in urban areas with tall buildings or uneven terrain, the nephoscope allows scientists to recognize obstacles disrupting ground-level wind patterns, enhancing understanding of wind behavior in complex environments.

NOW, THIS IS WILD!

Noctilucent clouds, meaning "night-shining" clouds, are Earth's highest, coldest, and rarest clouds. Appearing as ripples of gleaming silver and blue in the night sky, they form in the mesosphere layer of our atmosphere when light from the setting sun hits them. They occur when water vapor freezes into ice crystals that cling to dust particles left by falling meteors!

101

35

FEELING THE PRESSURE

You don't need to be a professional weather reporter to help predict the type of weather that's coming. By building a simple barometer, you can understand weather patterns and predict upcoming weather changes.

ESSENTIAL QUESTION

Can you build a device to predict upcoming pressure systems?

DIFFICULTY LEVEL: **Moderate**
SAFETY: ✂ ⚡

MATERIALS

- Scissors
- Uninflated balloon
- Large, empty glass jar
- Rubber bands
- Glue
- Bamboo skewer or plastic straws
- Paper
- Marker

PROCEDURE

1. Cut the neck of the balloon off, leaving the large round part.
2. Stretch the balloon over the mouth of the jar nice and tight. Use the rubber bands to secure the balloon in place. The tighter, the better—we don't want air to escape.
3. Place a glue strip on the balloon from the middle of the balloon to the edge. Press the bamboo skewer onto the glue with the pointy end away from the jar. (*See Figure I*) This will be the lever of your barometer. If you don't have a skewer, place one straw in another and glue it to the balloon. Depending on the glue, you may need to let it dry overnight.
4. Cut a strip of paper and make your gauge by adding a line in the middle. This will be your baseline. Then, mark every two millimeters above and below the baseline. This will help you determine if the pressure increases or decreases from the baseline.
5. Bring your barometer indoors out of direct sunlight and place it close to a wall. Tape the gauge behind the lever, setting the point at your baseline.
6. Record the skewer's position on the gauge daily in your science journal.

TAKE IT FURTHER

Pay attention to weather changes such as sunny, cloudy, rainy, or stormy days. Determine the relationship between atmospheric and weather patterns based on the movement of your barometer.

Figure I: Add a skewer onto the balloon.

NOW, THIS IS
WILL!

When lightning strikes, it creates heat five times hotter than the sun. This causes the air around the strike to heat rapidly, causing the air to expand. Immediately after the strike, the air cools and contracts so quickly that it creates a massive sound wave we hear as thunder.

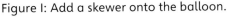

EXPLORE THE SCIENCE

Placing the balloon over the jar equalizes air pressure inside and outside. Weather changes alter external air pressure, affecting the balloon's surface pressure. In warm, nice weather, air pressure increases, pressing down on the balloon and raising the point on your lever. In bad weather, air pressure drops, causing the balloon to bulge outward and lowering the lever tip.

36

CLOUD CHAMBER

There are so many clouds in the sky, but how do they get there? In this activity, you'll uncover the science behind how clouds form by making your very own clouds.

ESSENTIAL QUESTION
How does a cloud form?

DIFFICULTY LEVEL: **Moderate**

SAFETY: 🔥

MATERIALS
- ¼ cup (60 ml) ice water
- Thermometer
- 2-liter soda bottles with caps (labels removed)
- Lighter
- Matches
- ¼ cup (60 ml) hot water (not boiling)

PROCEDURE
1. Record the temperature of the ice water in your science journal.
2. Pour the ice water into the soda bottle. Secure the cap and shake vigorously for 10 seconds.
3. With the soda bottle on a flat surface, ask a grown-up for help to remove the cap and drop a lighted match into the soda bottle. Replace the cap immediately.
4. Squeeze the soda bottle with both hands to increase the internal pressure, and remember what you observe so you can record it later in your science journal.
5. Now release the pressure by letting go of the bottle. Record both observations in your science journal. (*See Figure 1*) Continue squeezing, holding, and releasing, recording all observations in your science journal.
6. Record the temperature of the hot water in your science journal.
7. Pour the hot water into the second soda bottle. Secure the cap and shake vigorously.
8. Repeat steps 3 to 5 and record all observations in your science journal.

TAKE IT FURTHER
Track the air pressure on your barometer from Activity 35 and observe if a low-pressure system will create an uplift, causing the air to cool and expand, causing moisture to condense and form clouds.

Figure I: Squeeze the bottle to increase pressure, then release the pressure to see the cloud.

EXPLORE THE SCIENCE

The bottle with hot water best represents warm, moist conditions to create clouds. Squeezing the bottle increases air pressure, compressing the air. Upon release, pressure drops suddenly, causing rapid air expansion and cooling. This leads to condensation as cooled air can no longer hold as much moisture. Water vapor condenses around particles, forming cloudlike formations inside the bottle.

NOW, THIS IS WILD!

Scientists can make clouds produce more rain and snow in a process called cloud seeding! Using a plane, scientists add special chemicals like silver iodide and salt to clouds to help water droplets stick together and form more significant drops, which can fall as rain or snow! Cloud seeding helps clouds make more precipitation for places that need it.

105

PART 3
PHYSICAL SCIENCE

Physical science focuses on understanding the principles of the physical world and encompasses two main disciplines: physics and chemistry. Physics deals with concepts such as motion, forces, energy, and magnetism, whereas chemistry explores the composition and properties of matter. Physics and chemistry explain how the world around us works, significantly impacting technology and everyday applications, such as engineering, medicine, and materials science.

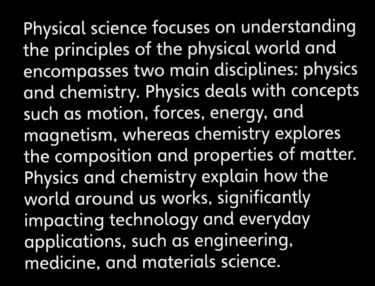
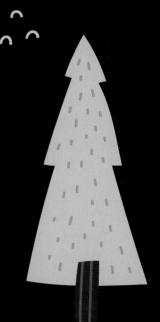

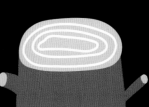

UNIT 10
ENERGY

As a young physicist, you'll explore applied physics, seeing energy in action! Energy drives change and transformations. For instance, think of turning on a light—to fill a room with brightness and warmth, electrical energy has to transform into light and heat energy. Learn about solar energy through art with Photograms. Impress your friends with Whirling Wonders, using secrets of centripetal force that almost seem magical. Test out the laws of motion when you build Chain Reactions to complete a simple task. Finally, explore potential and kinetic energy as you Crafting a Catapult, unlocking the secrets of physics and engineering!

37

PHOTOGRAMS

Have you ever taken pictures without a camera? This art form uses the sun's power and unique light-sensitive material to capture photographic images. Create stunning sun prints in this activity that preserve the intricate details of leaves, feathers, and more!

ESSENTIAL QUESTION

How can we use the sun's light energy to create unique prints?

DIFFICULTY LEVEL: **Moderate**

SAFETY: **!**

MATERIALS

- Natural items (leaves, ferns, flowers, grasses, pressed flowers, etc.)
- Cyanotype (sunprint) paper (found at a local craft store)
- Cardboard
- Plastic sheet
- Tape
- Bowl of water

PROCEDURE

1. Collect natural items for your prints. Leaves, feathers, flowers, and other flat specimens will produce more detailed images than bulky objects.
2. In a shady spot, place the cyanotype paper over cardboard. Arrange your objects on the cyanotype paper with the blue side facing up.
3. Cover the objects with a plastic sheet to hold everything in place. Secure the plastic sheet to the cardboard with tape.
4. Place your artwork in direct sunlight for 10 to 30 minutes. You should see the blue paper turn lighter. (*See Figure 1*)
5. When done, remove the natural objects and place the cyanotype paper in a bowl of water for 3 minutes, making sure it's completely covered with water.
6. Remove from water and allow to dry. (*See Figure 2*) You may need to press the paper in heavy books to flatten. Frame and hang!

TAKE IT FURTHER

Create a library of images around a theme for your books. Spring blooms, aquatic plants, evergreens, and ferns are just some ideas to start!

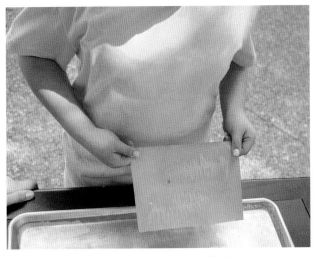

Figure 1: When the blue paper turns lighter, you can remove your objects.

EXPLORE THE SCIENCE

Cyanotype photography is a camera-less technique that uses paper coated with a light-sensitive solution. A specimen is placed directly onto dry paper and exposed to UV light for 10 to 40 minutes. The image is fixed by washing in water, appearing as a white negative on a blue (cyan) background. Architects and engineers widely use this process to create copies of plans, hence the term blueprint.

NOW, THIS IS WILD!

Anna Atkins (1799–1871) pioneered photograms (making images without a camera) to capture pictures of algae, ferns, and other plants. She was a botanist who was the first to illustrate a book with photographic images using the cyanotype process. You can see this book in the Natural History Museum online archives.

Figure 2: Remove your prints from the water and allow them to dry.

38

WHIRLING WONDERS

Explore the wonders of centripetal force in this activity as you amaze others by making water defy gravity.

ESSENTIAL QUESTION

What keeps the water in the container when it's suspended upside down over your head?

DIFFICULTY LEVEL: **Moderate**
SAFETY: ✂

MATERIALS
- Scissors
- Pizza box (or sturdy cardboard cut into a square)
- Duct tape
- Cotton string
- Plastic containers
- Water

PROCEDURE

1. Trim the sides off the pizza box, then tape the top and bottom together for sturdiness.
2. Make an "X" with string about double the length of your square with the extra hanging off the corners evenly. Tape the string securely to the square. (*See Figure 1*)
3. Flip the cardboard square and knot the ends of the string together, ensuring they are all equal in size.
4. Fill a plastic container with water and place at the square's center.
5. Be brave and swing the cardboard overhead in a circle, knowing you won't spill a drop on you! (*See Figure 2*)
6. Add more containers and challenge to see how many you can swing overhead. Record your observations in your science journal.

TAKE IT FURTHER

Stack cups or containers with cardboard in between and test your limits of using centripetal force to keep them balanced and not have the contents spill.

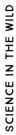

Figure 1: Tape the string across the box in an "X."

Figure 2: Swing the cardboard overhead.

EXPLORE THE SCIENCE

Swinging the platform in a circular motion pushes water outward, similar to the feeling of a car going around a sharp corner. This centripetal force pulls toward the circle's center. Swinging ropes around your head provides this force. Without this force, water would move in a straight line, spilling all over you.

NOW, THIS IS WILD!

Have you ever wondered why Earth just isn't traveling all around space? This is because of the pull of our sun's gravity. The centripetal force of gravity acts like a string, ensuring that Earth orbits in an elliptical loop rather than shooting off straight into the universe, which would turn us into an icy planet!

113

39

CHAIN REACTIONS

There's no more fun way to showcase energy and energy transfer principles than building a chain reaction machine. Get creative as you engineer a design to test crazy and wild sequences to complete an effortless task.

ESSENTIAL QUESTION

Can you construct a chain reaction device to complete a simple task?

DIFFICULTY LEVEL: **Advanced**
SAFETY: ➕

MATERIALS

- Pencil and paper
- Small sticks and twigs
- Stones
- String, yarn, long grasses, or vines
- Small cups or containers
- Any natural materials
- Any recyclable materials (cardboard, cans, paper roll tubes, buckets)

PROCEDURE

1. Designate a clear outdoor space free of obstacles or obstructions.
2. Decide what is the simple task that your chain reaction contraption will complete. Here are some ideas, or come up with some on your own:
    - water a flower
    - pop a water balloon
    - open the mailbox
    - launch a ball
3. Sketch your design to help choose materials, identify gaps, and discuss options for each section.
4. Start building! With a chain reaction machine, there is a lot of trial and error. One way to start may be with your end result and building your chain reaction backward. Another way to start is to build high, using gravity, like rocks in a bucket or an inclined plane, to start the reaction. (*See Figure 1*)
5. Do practice runs in segments so you can observe and see if adjustments are required. (*See Figure 2*)
6. Test the chain reaction and have fun! Be sure to record designs and observations in your science journal.

TAKE IT FURTHER

Grab some friends and challenge them to a build-off. Come up with a task everyone agrees on, then design, build, and test using your knowledge of physics, potential, and kinetic energy!

Figure 1: Add elements to your chain reaction.

NOW, THIS IS WILD!

Picture a skier swooshing down a mountain, sending a tiny tumble of snow rolling down, setting off one of nature's mega-chain reactions—an avalanche! An avalanche is a flowing sea of snow and air rapidly accelerating, capable of moving ice, large boulders, and full-grown trees!

Figure 2: Test steps of the reaction as you build it.

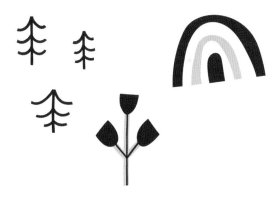

EXPLORE THE SCIENCE

Chain reaction devices showcase transforming potential or stored energy into kinetic energy or motion. Energy transfer occurs as one action imparts energy to the next, demonstrating how various forms interact to produce a series of linked movements or tasks in fun and intricate ways.

40

CRAFTING A CATAPULT

Learn about the fascinating principles of physics and engineering while you design, build, and test your catapults to launch projectiles.

ESSENTIAL QUESTION
Can you build a catapult to launch marshmallows over a set distance?

DIFFICULTY LEVEL: **Moderate**
SAFETY:

MATERIALS
- 6 sticks or bamboo rods of equal length (about 1 yard [1 m])
- Single hole punch
- Plastic cup
- 10–12 large rubber bands
- Scissors
- String
- Large marshmallows or table tennis balls
- Target (optional)

PROCEDURE

1. Use three sticks or bamboo rods to build the base of the catapult. Place them into a triangle and secure each corner with string.
2. To complete the frame, which supports the catapult's action, take the other three sticks or bamboo rods and create a pyramid shape. Secure each stick to a corner of the base with a string, then join them with string at the top. (*See Figure 1*)
3. Create the catapult bucket by punching three single holes around the top of the cup. Be sure to keep them spaced evenly apart.
4. Use three to four large rubber bands to make an elastic band arm by looping rubber bands together. Make three arms and secure each to the holes in the cup. (*See Figure 2*)
5. Secure one rubber band arm to the top of the frame and secure the others to two bottom corners of the frame. (*See Figure 3*)
6. Launch your bucket by placing the marshmallow (or table tennis ball) in the cup, pulling it back on the cup to create tension, and then releasing the bucket. Observe how far the marshmallow launches. Set up a target and challenge yourself to hit the mark!

TAKE IT FURTHER
Make modifications to your catapult to see if you can increase the tension for heavier loads, launch heavier projectiles by making a more robust bucket, or create a more secure frame and see the greatest distance you can launch.

Figure I: Use string or secure frame at corners.

Figure 2: Use rubber bands to create three arms.

Figure 3: Secure the arms to the base and top of the frame.

EXPLORE THE SCIENCE

A catapult is a device that uses tension or torsion to launch projectiles. The catapult works when the stored elastic potential energy in the stretched rubber bands is converted to kinetic energy when they snap back upon release, moving the bucket and launching the projectile. The more stored energy, the farther the projectile will go.

NOW, THIS IS WILD!

Have you ever seen a pumpkin hurling 4,438 feet (I,353 meters) across the sky? It's wild! This launch holds the world record for pumpkin chunking. Since 1986, the pumpkin has been rocketed into the sky by different launching devices, such as catapults, at the World Championship Punkin Chunkin event, where "backyard engineers" hurl pumpkins through the air without electricity or explosives.

UNIT 11
MATTER

It's the little things that matter, literally, when you're a young particle physicist. Matter is anything that has mass and takes up space, which includes anything you can touch, see, smell, and even those you can't, like air. Discover properties of water and soap when making Square Bubbles. Uncover a Secret Message through chemical reactions and pH levels. Witness phase changes as you turn natural materials into stunning Ice Lanterns. Learn about mixing matter in Mingle Inn, and build a cozy home for our six-legged friends because they matter too!

41

SQUARE BUBBLES

Let's explore bubbles with a twist—square bubbles! By examining soapy water's properties and geometry, you will challenge the conventional round bubble by creating mesmerizing cube-shaped bubbles.

ESSENTIAL QUESTION

How do the sides of a cube-shaped bubble wand help make a square bubble?

DIFFICULTY LEVEL: **Moderate**
SAFETY: !

MATERIALS
- Bucket
- ¼ cup (85 g) liquid dish soap
- 4 cups (940 ml) water
- 2 teaspoons glycerin (optional)
- Pipe cleaners or bendable wire
- Drinking straw

PROCEDURE
1. Mix the dish soap and water in the bucket. If you have some, add glycerin, allowing the bubbles to last longer.
2. Use the bendable wire to make a bubble wand into a square shape. Dip it in the bubble solution, lift it out, and blow through it. Record your observations.
3. Now construct a cube using pipe cleaners (or wire, or even plastic toys used for building). (*See Figure I*)
4. Dip the cube in the bubble mixture and pull it out slowly. If a square does not instantly appear in the center, dip your straw into the bubble mixture and gently blow a bubble into the middle of the cube. Record your observations.

TAKE IT FURTHER
Try making other 3D bubble wands, such as pyramids or hexagons, and see if they create different-shaped bubbles.

Figure 1: Bend the pipe cleaners in the shape of a cube.

NOW, THIS IS
WILD!

EXPLORE THE SCIENCE

Blowing bubbles with a two-dimensional wand results in round bubbles due to water's surface tension. When air is blown into the soapy solution, it stretches equally on all sides, forming a sphere. Using a cube-shaped (3D) wand creates multiple bubbles around the center. While the center bubble wants to become a sphere, pressure from the other bubbles pushes against it on all sides, forming the cube shape!

Many artists are masters of bubbles, trying to push the limits of what they can do. In 2021, Su Chang-Tai achieved a world record by blowing 1,339 bubbles inside one giant bubble! Try it yourself and see how many you can do!

42

SECRET MESSAGE

DIFFICULTY LEVEL: **Moderate**

SAFETY: !

MATERIALS

- 1 tablespoon (14 g) baking soda (sodium bicarbonate)
- ½ cup (120 ml) water
- 2 containers
- 2 plastic spoons
- 1 teaspoon turmeric
- ½ cup (120 ml) rubbing alcohol
- Small paintbrush or cotton swab
- Paper
- Large paintbrush

Ever wanted to be a spy and send secret messages? You can craft hidden messages using chemical reactions by exploring the fascinating science of pH and natural indicators.

ESSENTIAL QUESTION

What secrets can you reveal using chemical reactions?

PROCEDURE

1. Add one tablespoon (14 g) of baking soda to the water in one container. Stir with a plastic spoon. Not all the baking soda will dissolve.
2. Be sure you're outdoors for this step because it has a strong odor, and ask a grown-up if you need help. In the second container, add one teaspoon of turmeric to the rubbing alcohol. Stir with the other plastic spoon.
3. Use a small paintbrush or cotton swab to write your secret messages on paper using the baking soda solution. (*See Figure 1*) Lay the paper out in the sun to dry.
4. When the message is dry, dip the large paintbrush into the turmeric solution and paint across the paper, revealing the message. (*See Figure 2*) Record your observations in your science journal.

TAKE IT FURTHER

Try using other natural pH indicators to reveal secret messages, such as cabbage juice, grape juice, curry powder, turnip skins, and cherries.

Figure 2: Paint across the paper to reveal the message.

Figure I: Paint the secret message with baking soda.

EXPLORE THE SCIENCE

Baking soda, a base with a pH higher than 7 on an acid-base scale, remains colorless when applied and dried on paper. Turmeric, a natural pH indicator, contains curcumin that changes color in the presence of substances with different pH levels. When the turmeric solution reacts with the baking soda on paper, the curcumin changes color from yellow to reddish-brown, revealing the hidden message.

NOW, THIS IS WILL!

Animals send their own hidden messages using a chemical substance called pheromones. Pheromones are unique scents that send silent messages only their friends can reveal, telling them about food, danger, or a new place everyone can move to.

43

ICE LANTERNS

Embark on a botanical treasure hunt, seeking unique shapes, scents, and colors found in nature to adorn enchanting ice lanterns that highlight the beauty of the outdoors.

ESSENTIAL QUESTION

How do impurities in frozen water help create a magical nighttime light display?

DIFFICULTY LEVEL: **Easy**
SAFETY: 🔥

MATERIALS
- Small natural items (berries, pine needles, small acorns, seed pods, etc.)
- Water
- Bucket (optional)
- 12-inch (30 cm) balloon
- Bowl (optional)
- Votive candles

PROCEDURE

1. On a winter day, hunt to find botanical treasures. Look for unique shapes like seed pods, smells like juniper and rosemary needles, and colors found in berries and leaves to use in your ice lanterns.
2. Stretch the opening of a balloon and carefully add the items.
3. Fill the balloon with water and tie off the balloon. Note: If filling your balloons indoors, use a bucket to transfer them outdoors to prevent breaking and making a mess!
4. If it's below 32°F (0°C), you can leave your water balloons outdoors to freeze overnight. If not, carefully place it in your freezer in a bowl. (*See Figure 1*)
5. The next day, remove the balloon by tearing it away from the ice. You will notice you have a flat side. Break the ice on the flat side to find a hollow area. (*See Figure 2*)
6. Place a votive candle inside and enjoy the beautiful ice lanterns.

TAKE IT FURTHER

Create several lanterns to line a walkway or driveway. Try experimenting with colored water to make your lanterns festive.

Figure I: Freeze the water balloons.

Figure 2: Break the ice on the flat side to reveal the hollow center.

EXPLORE THE SCIENCE

The water in an ice balloon freezes from the outside in. As the water freezes, impurities such as air and minerals are left behind in the liquid, where they concentrate and come out of the solution as bubbles. These tiny bubbles will not only help scatter your lantern's light but are concentrated enough to allow the inside to be hollowed for the votive candle.

NOW, THIS IS WILD!

Kungur Ice Cave in Perm Krai, Russia, was discovered in 1703. This cave is rare because it features a full range of climatic zones, with the entrance staying in a zone of permanent freezing temperatures that provide fantastic ice formations that visitors around the world come to enjoy!

44

MINGLE INN

Making a bug hotel is an interactive way to explore mixtures. In this activity, you'll observe, experiment, and understand how different materials come together to create habitats for bugs.

ESSENTIAL QUESTION

Which mixture of materials makes the best home for bugs?

DIFFICULTY LEVEL: **Easy**
SAFETY: 🐾

MATERIALS

All optional, use what you can find
- Recycled wooden box or crate
- Hollow materials (bamboo canes, plant stems)
- Straw hay
- Wood (twigs, loose bark, dry sticks, rotting wood, wood chips)
- Stones
- Pinecones
- Recycled material (bricks, pots, cardboard, popsicle sticks)
- Twine
- Chicken wire (optional)
- Stapler (optional)
- Magnifying glass

PROCEDURE

1. If your wooden box does not have compartments, make some using recycled pieces of wood or large pieces of loose bark that fit firmly in place.
2. Start filling compartments with materials. (*See Figure 1*) Hollow bamboo shelters solitary bees, and straw and small twigs provide good hiding spots. Small stones mixed with soil allow bugs to burrow.
3. Layer the materials in each compartment, ensuring a mix of textures and sizes. Pack the materials tightly to create stable and secure habitats.
4. Once sections are filled, you can secure the hotel by stapling chicken wire on it or attaching it firmly to a fence or tree to avoid falling in the wind.
5. Place your bug hotel in a designated spot, like a garden or near vegetation. Monitor daily and add fresh materials if needed, making sure to mark your observations in your science journal. Use a magnifying glass to take a closer look at your inn's residents.

TAKE IT FURTHER

Create other bug hotels and place them in various locations. Compare and contrast the bug species that visit, and determine their behavior and preferences.

Figure I: Use materials like rocks, pinecones, bamboo, and sticks to create a bug hotel in a container, like this broken cardboard cat scratcher.

EXPLORE THE SCIENCE

Bug hotels require maintenance, and the mixtures of soil, leaves, twigs, stones, and other natural and recycled materials might change, demonstrating how mixtures can be dynamic. Bug hotels allow observers to see which bugs are attracted to specific layers or see if some layers are used for nesting while others provide food.

NOW, THIS IS WILD!

A team of seven people were involved in construction of the largest bug hotel which boasts a size of 200 cubic meters—or imagine a fish tank that holds 52,800 gallons (200 kiloliters) of water! This bug hotel took six months to complete and is being enjoyed by insects around Scotland!

FORCE AND MOTION

As a young mechanical physicist, explore force and motion through experiments to understand and manipulate motion. Force—the push or pull that causes objects to change speed or direction—and motion—the change in position over time—are central. Increase tensile strength in grass by making Grass Ropes. Uncover magnetic forces in Sand's Magnetic Charm. Design a zipline in the Zipline Challenge, and maybe you can use it to have someone send you some snacks as you're working. Create unique works of art with sand in Pendulum Patterns. Force and motion come together as you design some seriously cool stuff!

45

GRASS ROPES

Unravel the secrets behind the durability of natural fibers by pulling, stretching, and investigating the tensile strength hidden within ropes made of grass.

ESSENTIAL QUESTION

What factors contribute to the ability of grass to withstand pulling forces?

DIFFICULTY LEVEL: **Moderate**
SAFETY: ✂ ✚

MATERIALS

- Source for long grass that is not too dry to avoid breakage
- Ruler
- Grass clippers or scissors to collect the grass

PROCEDURE

1. Make multiple bundles of long grass all the same diameter; approximately ⅔-inch (1.5 cm) diameter works well for beginners.
2. To start your rope, grab one bundle and use both hands to twist the bundle in the middle. (*See Figure 1*)
3. Once you have about 3 inches (7–8 cm) twisted, fold the bundle in half and continue to twist both ends. You should notice that the bundle wraps into a rope while twisting. (*See Figure 2*)
4. When your hands start feeling the ends of the bundle, you'll have to splice in new grass to continue to make your rope. Do this by grabbing two new bundles, laying them on top of each end of the original strand, and continuing to twist. (*See Figure 3*) The new strands will weave into the rope. It's important to keep both strands of your rope the same diameter.
5. Continue to add bundles until your rope is the desired length.
6. Tie the two loose ends with a square knot to secure your rope. Use your rope to lift objects or test its strength in a game of tug of war with your family or friends.

TAKE IT FURTHER

Get a group of friends and use larger bundles of grass to build different lengths and sizes of ropes that you can use to pull, test, and play games with.

Figure I: Twist a handful of grass to start the rope.

Figure 2: Fold the bundle in half and make a loop while twisting.

Figure 3: Splice in new grass to make the rope longer.

EXPLORE THE SCIENCE

To turn grass into rope involves understanding the tensile strength, a.k.a. the material's resistance to breaking under tension. Grass stems consist of long, fibrous cells that, when twisted together, create friction, interlocking to form a rope that resists breaking when pulled.

NOW, THIS IS WILD!

Known as the last remaining suspension bridge made of grass, the Q'eswachaka bridge has been built and rebuilt continuously by the people of Peru for five centuries. Every spring, the Quechua women and men twist grass into rope and then braid it into thick cables that will be used to construct this 110-foot (30 m) walking bridge!

46

SAND'S MAGNETIC CHARM

Magnetism is a physical property of matter found in interesting objects like sand. Use your observation skills to uncover how various sands interact with magnets.

ESSENTIAL QUESTION

Can you determine if different sand samples have magnetic properties?

DIFFICULTY LEVEL: **Easy**

SAFETY: !

MATERIALS

- Sand samples (beach, sandy soil, or playground)
- Small cup
- Clean container
- Strong magnet
- Sandwich bag

PROCEDURE

1. Collect and label sand samples from multiple sources. Be sure it is as clean as possible of any debris.
2. Fill the small cup with your first sample of sand and pour it into a clean container.
3. Place your magnet into a sandwich bag and seal it to prevent particles from sticking to your magnet during the investigation.
4. Hold the magnet over the sand sample without touching it. Slowly move the magnet closer to the sand, making observations. (*See Figure 1*) Record any attraction of magnetite, a magnetic sand particle, to your magnet. (*See Figure 2*)
5. Place the magnet in the sand and see how much magnetite you can pull from the first sample. Record your findings in your science journal.
6. Repeat steps 2 to 5 with all the sand samples, cleaning the container between each sample. Compare each sample and record your observations.

TAKE IT FURTHER

Use a magnifying lens to discover all the different materials that make up sand. Compare the size, color, and shape of grains among your samples. Look for yellow and pink feldspar, shiny translucent mica, or even bits of beach glass.

Figure 1: Run a magnet inside a baggie through sand.

Figure 2: Observe what was pulled from the sand.

EXPLORE THE SCIENCE

Sand comes from once-living organisms like coral or nonliving components like rock. Mostly derived from the breakdown of the continental crust, sand often contains quartz, feldspar, mica, and magnetite. The black sand attracted to magnets is magnetite, a naturally occurring iron oxide mineral.

NOW, THIS IS WILD!

Did you know that the beautiful white beaches of Hawaii are made of poop? That's right—parrotfish poop! Parrotfish have powerful beaks that scrape and nibble on algae from chunks of dead coral. Once swallowed, the parrotfish grind up the inedible coral skeletons in their gut, then poop it out as white sand.

133

47

ZIPLINE CHALLENGE

Seeing forces of gravity and friction in action is incredible, especially when those forces bring you a treat. In this activity, you'll create a zipline to send treats zooming to the other side using your physics and engineering skills.

ESSENTIAL QUESTION
How does the angle of descent affect the speed of a zipline?

DIFFICULTY LEVEL: **Easy**
SAFETY: ✂

MATERIALS
- Paper cup
- Scissors or hole punch
- String
- Toilet paper or paper towel rolls
- Tape
- Materials to decorate (markers, stickers, tissue paper, etc.)

PROCEDURE
1. Create a basket for your zipline by punching two holes in the rim of the paper cup.
2. Cut a piece of string and make a handle by tying each end securely to the holes. Be sure the handle can fit around the toilet paper roll (trolley) and that there is enough room to place things in the basket.
3. Tape the handle of the basket to the toilet paper roll. Decorate your basket if you wish.
4. Find a suitable location between two sturdy points (trees, poles, porch railing) to place your zipline.
5. Securely tie the string to one point.
6. Measure how long your string needs to be to reach the other point, making sure to add extra since the string will need to be secured higher than the other side.
7. Before securing your string, slide the end of it through the toilet paper roll. Once through the roll, attach the string taut so the cable has no slack. (*See Figure 1*)
8. Place snacks or lightweight items in the bucket, then release the toilet paper roll on the higher end of the zipline and observe how it slides down while carrying items to the other side. (*See Figure 2*) Draw a diagram of your zipline in your science journal and make any notes on adjustments.

TAKE IT FURTHER
Experiment by adjusting the slope of the zipline or adding weights to the cup to observe their effect on speed and stability. If bucket contents fly out, use a pool noodle at the end to create a bumper!

Figure I: Add a toilet roll trolley to the zipline.

Figure 2: Release the toilet paper roll on the zipline.

EXPLORE THE SCIENCE

A zipline uses gravity to pull an object down an inclined cable. As the object descends, its potential energy turns to kinetic energy, propelling it forward. Friction between the trolley and the cable, along with factors like cable tension and the angle of descent, control the speed of the carried object.

How would you like to zipline to school? Well, that's exactly what some kids living in Colombia's rural parts do. Every morning, they hook onto a cable system and take a thrilling ride between trees to get to school, enabling them to traverse valleys and rugged terrain quickly and safely.

NOW, THIS IS WILD!

48. PENDULUM PATTERNS

Ever wonder if gravity could be your artist's assistant? In this activity, you'll create mesmerizing patterns by letting gravity and other forces in nature guide the flow of sand into unique masterpieces.

ESSENTIAL QUESTION
Can you create art using gravity?

DIFFICULTY LEVEL: **Moderate**
SAFETY: ✂ ✚

MATERIALS
- Large water bottle
- Nail
- Hammer
- Scissors
- Cotton string
- Large black tablecloth, or dark construction paper
- Masking tape
- Light-colored sand
- Food coloring

PROCEDURE
1. Ask for a grown-up's help to use a nail to punch three holes evenly spaced apart about 2 inches (5 cm) from the bottom of the water bottle. Use the hammer and nail to also make a hole in the center of the bottle cap.
2. Use scissors to cut off the bottom of the water bottle about ½ inch (1 cm) above the holes.
3. Cut three 10-inch (25 cm) pieces of string. Tie each one securely at each hole.
4. Cut a 6½-foot (2 m) piece of string and tie the short pieces to it. This is now your support string.
5. Secure your support string over a flat area. (*See Figure 1*) The flat areas could be a branch, a garage doorway, an archway, or a broomstick suspended between two trees.
6. Lay out your tablecloth, or tape your construction paper to make a canvas.
7. Place a piece of tape over the hole in your lid, then add sand to your bottle. Add food coloring, then layer the sand in the bottle for a dramatic effect.
8. Pull the bottle slightly off to one side, remove the tape, and release it over your canvas. Record your observations of your sand art.
9. Carefully collect sand and start over.

TAKE IT FURTHER
Attach the support string to an additional horizontal support string. If you change the length of the horizontal string, you will get amazing patterns.

Figure I: Secure your support string.

EXPLORE THE SCIENCE

When the pendulum is pulled to one side and released, gravity pulls it toward its resting position, while inertia (the property of an object to resist change in motion) makes it move in a straight line. These two forces cause a swinging pendulum to create an elliptical path, as shown by the sand.

NOW, THIS IS WILD!

Swings are giant pendulums. If you ever find yourself in Queensland, New Zealand, you can ride the largest swing in the world—the Nevis Swing. This thrill ride flings the rider in an arc more than 1,000 feet (300 meters) over a canyon!

137

UNIT 13

WAVES

Waves are like invisible messengers carrying energy through air, water, and space. They are the reason we can hear music and see colors and are used in radio communication and X-rays for medical imaging. As a young optics and acoustic physicist, you'll send sound waves through the air with the help of your own Awesome Aerophones. Use vibrations to become the ultimate Worm Charmer. Turn the ordinary into the extraordinary as you add a splash of shifting colors in Iridescence Rocks. Finally, be mesmerized by the display of vibrant and swirling colors in the Polarizing Palette. Now, go out there and make some waves!

Making musical instruments is a fun way to investigate sound. In this activity, you will create two simple instruments and compare the differences in the sound waves they produce.

ESSENTIAL QUESTION

How do different vibrations create various sounds?

DIFFICULTY LEVEL: **Easy**

SAFETY: ✂ ✚

MATERIALS

- Hammer and nail
- Paint stir stick or wooden ruler
- Two 24-inch (60 cm) long pieces of thick string or yarn
- Metal hanger
- Wide rubber bands

PROCEDURE

Part I: Bullroarer

1. Use a hammer and nail to punch a hole in the stir stick about I inch (2.5 cm) from the end.
2. Tie one end through the hole and make a knot, securing the string.
3. Hold the string about I foot (30 cm) down on the string and swing it around like a lasso. (*See Figure I*) You may have to adjust where you hold the string to find the sweet spot to make the "roar."

Part 2: Buzzing Bee

4. While holding the top of the hanger, pull on the bottom until you have made a square.
5. Place 2 to 3 rubber bands across the square hanger, all in the same direction.
6. Tie the string around the handle of the hanger, then bend the handle close so the string doesn't slip off.
7. Repeat step 3 from Part I, listening for the "buzz" like a bee.

TAKE IT FURTHER

Try making different musical instruments with everyday materials, such as rubber bands as strings or plastic tops as drums.

Figure I: Swing the aerophone like a lasso to hear the sounds.

EXPLORE THE SCIENCE

Aerophones are musical instruments that vibrate the air to make sound. Sound is created by waves that can be big or small and have different wavelengths. The bigger the wave, the louder the sound. Longer wavelengths, or slower vibrations, make low-pitched sounds, while faster vibrations make high-pitched sounds.

NOW, THIS IS WILD!

Elephants communicate through vibrations that can travel in the air and ground. They produce infrasonic rumbles too low for humans to hear that can travel for miles, allowing elephants to "talk" with each other across long distances, maintaining social connections within their herds.

50.

WORM CHARMER

Worm charming is the art of coaxing worms to the surface. In this activity, let's see if you can mimic the natural warning signals that would prompt these underground dwellers to emerge from the soil.

ESSENTIAL QUESTION

How do vibrations impact worms' behavior?

PROCEDURE

1. Find a suitable area with moist soil, preferably in a shaded spot, where worms are likely present.
2. Push the garden rake tines into the soil.
3. Hammer a large stick into the ground. (*Figure I*) Rub it across the back of the tines, generating vibrations. Continue this rubbing motion for several minutes, maintaining the vibrations through the ground.
4. Pay attention to the vibrations felt through the handle of the rake. These vibrations mimic those produced by mole movements or rainfall, prompting the worms to surface.
5. As worms emerge from the soil, collect them gently and count how many surface. Record your observations in your science journal. Return the worms to the same area when you're done.

TAKE IT FURTHER

Try different objects to create vibrations and see if you can lure more worms to the surface. Try several locations to see if one area is better than another for worm charming.

DIFFICULTY LEVEL: **Easy**
SAFETY: 🐾

MATERIALS

- Small garden rake or trowel
- Hammer
- Large stick

SCIENCE IN THE WILD

Figure I: Hammer the stick in the ground to create vibrations.

EXPLORE THE SCIENCE

Worms possess sensory structures called setae, which are sensitive to vibrations in the soil. Worm charming mimics vibrations similar to moles hunting for worms underground. In response to these vibrations, the setae help worms interpret them as a signal of potential danger from a predator and move closer to the surface, using this warning system to avoid being a mole's lunch.

NOW, THIS IS WILD!

Sophie Smith holds the record for charming 567 worms in 30 minutes during the World Worm Charming Competition in the United Kingdom. Using a traditional method of wiggling and hitting a fork in the ground to create vibrations, she coaxed the worms out, achieving this astonishing feat at age 10!

143

51

IRIDESCENCE ROCKS

Iridescence is a natural phenomenon seen in feathers, seashell nacre, minerals, and arthropod exoskeletons that allow certain surfaces to change color at different angles. In this activity, you'll transform ordinary surfaces into brilliant, colorful ones.

ESSENTIAL QUESTION

Can you turn ordinary rocks into an iridescent display of rainbows?

DIFFICULTY LEVEL: **Easy**

SAFETY: !

MATERIALS

- Container
- Water
- Clear nail polish
- Dark rocks (smooth and rough edges)
- Other natural items (pinecones, acorns, etc.)

PROCEDURE

1. Fill your container with water deep enough for your rocks to be submerged.
2. When the water surface is still, hold the nail polish brush close to the water and drip 1 to 2 drops of nail polish onto the surface. The polish will spread.
3. Choose a smooth rock, submerge it under the water where there is NO nail polish, and pull it back up through the surface where there IS nail polish. The film of nail polish will stick to the rock. (*See Figure 1*)
4. Repeat steps 2 to 3 with a rock with rough edges or some other natural items, and pull the ragged edge up through the nail polish. Check out those fantastic colors! (*See Figure 2*)
5. Lay your rocks out to dry. Compare the rocks and record your observations in your science journal.

TAKE IT FURTHER

Make iridescent bookmarks using black construction paper. Cut paper into strips and use the same technique. Just be sure to let the paper lay out to dry!

Figure 1: Pull a rock through the clear nail polish floating on top of the water.

Figure 2: Observe the iridescence on the rock.

EXPLORE THE SCIENCE

Iridescence occurs when colors shift as the viewing angle changes, often caused by thin film interference. The clear nail polish forms a super thin layer similar to a soap film and reflects light differently due to variations in its thickness. Observe how the rough edges show the iridescence more due to the increased angles of reflections.

NOW, THIS IS WILD!

The blue morpho butterfly's wings are entirely colorless. However, because the wings are blanketed in translucent scales (about 600 per square millimeter), some rays of light bounce off top-level scales, while some light goes through and reflects off of lower levels, causing interference, giving the wings magnificently iridescent blue coloring.

52

POLARIZING PALETTE

Light waves are all around us. In this activity, explore how light and a special film work together to create stunning masterpieces that change right before your eyes.

ESSENTIAL QUESTION

How do light waves change when passing through layers of polarizing film?

DIFFICULTY LEVEL: **Moderate**
SAFETY: ✂

MATERIALS

- Polarizing film sheet cut into squares
- Clear plastic from packaging
- Scissors
- Packing tape, or other transparent tape
- Brass fastener

PROCEDURE

1. Cut the clear plastic to the same size as your polarizing film sheet.
2. Cut tape strips into different lengths and shapes, and stick them to the plastic sheet. Make a random design or a creative pattern—the more the tape overlaps, the better the polarizing effect. (*See Figure 1*)
3. Place the plastic sheet in between the two pieces of film. Use the scissors to make a hole through the center of all three layers big enough for a brass fastener to fit through.
4. Insert the brass fastener to secure the layers. (*See Figure 2*)
5. Hold your polarized art up to the sunlight and rotate the top piece of film to enjoy your masterpiece.

TAKE IT FURTHER

Place other clear plastic items between the two polarizing films to see how light is bent and travels through them, changing speed and color.

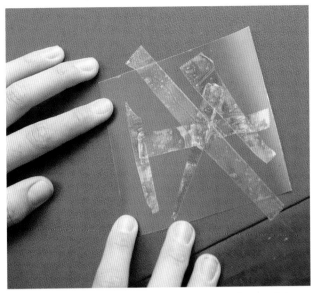

Figure I: Add strips of clear tape on one sheet of the polarizing film.

Figure 2: Attach the top sheet of polarizing film using a brass fastener.

EXPLORE THE SCIENCE

The first polarizing film allows light to pass through in one direction. Plastic and tape between the films break the sunlight into different colors. Reflected colored light from the tape passes through the second polarizing film only when aligned with the first filter's slits. If the colored light does not line up, it is blocked, only allowing some light through, creating different colors as the film is rotated.

NOW, THIS IS **WILD!**

Scientists are turning microscopy images into polarized works of art! Crystals made by vitamin C, aspirin and even dried tears, viewed and photographed through light microscopes, can display the most intense and beautiful colors just by adding polarized film over the light source and placing another in the eye piece.

147

ACKNOWLEDGMENTS

I extend my deepest gratitude to the incredible team at Quarry Books for their unwavering support and dedication throughout this journey. Jonathan, Elizabeth, and Heather, your guidance and expertise have been invaluable, and I am truly grateful for the opportunity to work with such talented individuals.

I would like to extend my sincere appreciation to Teresa for capturing all the incredible moments during this project and adding so much joy to our photoshoot days. Your kindness, dedication, and talent have made every moment unforgettable for everyone.

To my cherished friends Cindy and Melanie—your enthusiasm and willingness to join in on the adventure have made this experience even more memorable. Thank you both, along with Rachel, Jenni, Kristi, and Jimmy, for always being up for fun and graciously sharing your amazing and beautiful kiddos for the photoshoot.

A heartfelt shoutout to my ride-or-die team, Erin and Bethany. Your steadfast loyalty and unwavering support have been a constant source of strength on this wild rollercoaster ride. Thank you for never hesitating to stand by my side, no matter what twists and turns come our way.

To Dan, my eternal copilot in this crazy adventure we call life, thanks for always taking the wheel—literally and figuratively—because, let's face it, my navigation skills are questionable at best. You never flinch when I ask you to hop fences through prickers for seeds, head out to hunt for scorpions, or watch me walk in with *another* plant from the nursery. Here's to many more hilarious detours and unforgettable memories ahead!

To my little squad—Ava, Dani, and Lincoln—you bring so much joy and purpose into my life. Your laughs, playful attitudes, and amazing imaginations keep me in constant awe. I love you all the way to Betelgeuse and back!

To the rest of my family and friends who have supported me through this project—your encouragement means everything.

And to the naturally curious young scientists who enjoy this book and make all this possible: Thank you for making the future look so bright!

ABOUT THE AUTHOR

Dr. Erica Colón, a distinguished educator and author, is recognized for her influential work in science curriculum and instruction. With extensive experience as a National Board-Certified teacher across various science disciplines, she prioritizes student engagement. In 2012, she founded Nitty Gritty Science, LLC, creating and distributing acclaimed science resources globally. Dr. Colón also shares valuable insights and engaging content on social media platforms such as TikTok, Instagram, and Facebook under the handle @nittygrittyscience.

Dr. Colón loves taking road trips with her family, always seeking new adventures. She coaches her kids' sports teams, loves trying new recipes, and loves hunting for antique microscopes at auctions. Whenever there is downtime, you will find her curled up with her cat and dog, Newton and Einstein, enjoying epic movies or good books.

FOREST IS MY HAPPY PLACE

INDEX

ADVENTURE

EXPLORE